OHIO

OHIO

The Spirit of América

Text by Diana Landau

Harry N. Abrams, Inc., Publishers

NEW YORK

This series was originated by Walking Stick Press, San Francisco
Series Designer: Linda Herman; Series Editor: Diana Landau

Editor: Nicole Columbus
Designer: Ana Rogers

Photo research: Laurie Platt Winfrey, Van Bucher, Carousel Research, Inc.

Page 1: *Milking Time* by Nancy Cones Ford, 1912. *American Heritage*
Page 2: *Ella's Hotel, Richfield Center, Ohio* by Otto Bacher, 1885. *Manoogian Collection*

Library of Congress Cataloguing-in-Publication Data
Landau, Diana, 1950–
    Ohio : the spirit of America / text by Diana Landau.
    p.   cm.
    ISBN 0–8109–5572–5
    1. Ohio—Civilization—Miscellanea.   2. Ohio—Description and travel—
Miscellanea.   3. Ohio—Pictorial works.   I. Title.

F491 .L27 2001
977.1—dc21   2001018826

Harry N. Abrams, Inc.
100 Fifth Avenue
New York, N.Y. 10011
www.abramsbooks.com

Amish quilt, in a variation of the log cabin pattern, from Holmes County, late 19th century.

Christie's Images

CONTENTS

> *"Ohio is the farthest west of the east and the farthest north of the south."*
>
> Louis Bromfield, Pulitzer Prize—winning Ohio novelist

Ohio lacks almost nothing except an instantly recognizable symbol—perhaps because Ohio is not one thing but all things American, not distinctly north, south, east, or west but some of each. By a happy collision of geography and history, it became a crossroads for the young nation. As its legacy, Ohio got the industriousness and cultural polish of the northern and eastern states, the South's profound respect for tradition, and the restless energy that blazed trails across the western frontier. This also helps explain why eight Ohioans have been elected U.S. president. People from all over the country can see something of themselves in a leader from Ohio.

From the start Ohio was blessed in its land, perhaps even more in its waters. It is sandwiched by two great navigation systems: the Great Lakes to the north and the Ohio River on its southern border. While the Ohio brought settlers in, the Great Lakes carried goods, from furs to steel, out of the heart of the continent. Some of those settlers went on to the Mississippi and beyond, but many left their flatboats to make their way up the Ohio's tributaries and claim farmsteads.

As they cleared the land, settlers uncovered evidence of prehistoric villages and burial mounds containing some of the finest decorative arts made east of Mexico. In the familiar tale of takeover, settlers and their military back-up also drove out the tribes that lived lightly in the forest: the Shawnee,

Ohio Valley and Kentucky Hills **by Lewis Henry Meakin, 1910.** *Courtesy Proctor & Gamble, Cincinnati*

Miami, and others. Ohio's soil, once broken, proved incredibly fertile, thanks to the glacier that ages earlier dragged sediments over the landscape. The new Ohioans, proliferating after statehood in 1803, soon made theirs the leading farm state and founded industries based on farm products. When they lost their edge in agriculture, Ohioans discovered and exploited riches beneath the soil: goodly deposits of coal, oil, natural gas, stone, and pottery clay.

Horsedrawn Cart in Thunderstorm by William Sommer, 1918.
Collection of Joseph M. and Elsie Erdelac

Ohio is still a farming as well as an industrial state. Growing up along the abundant rivers, canals, roads, and railways, it became a state of small towns and modest-sized cities. Not for Ohio one overweening metropolis like Chicago; rather, half-a-dozen urban centers share the wealth. Much of Ohio's life still goes on in small towns like the aptly named Charm, in the heart of Amish country; Marietta, a well- preserved Ohio River landing; and Chagrin Falls in the Western Reserve, where New England settlers left their stamp on local architecture and customs.

Ohioans are demonstrably industrious, but they are just as good at having fun. They fervently support their Ohio State Buckeyes as well as two major-league baseball teams, two NFL squads, and an NBA team. They are found by the thousands on the golf course on any fine weekend. Or flocking to their spectacular theme parks, their big-time state fair, to Akron's nostalgic Soap Box Derby or the verdant lawn of Blossom Music Center, the Cleveland Orchestra's summer home. Besides these attractions, Ohio has practically cornered the market on "halls of fame": Cleveland's Rock & Roll Hall of Fame and the Football Hall of Fame in Canton top the list.

There should be a Great Ohioans hall of fame, too. In addition to its eight presidents, Ohio has produced generals George Armstrong Custer, Ulysses S. Grant (also president), and William Tecumseh Sherman (not to mention the original Tecumseh); athletes Jesse Owens and Cy Young; industrialists John D. Rockefeller and George Steinbrenner; and countless stage, screen, and recording idols. Roy Rogers practiced his riding and Annie Oakley her sharpshooting in their home state; inventors Thomas Edison and the Wright Brothers began their tinkering here. Cincinnati, known as Porkopolis in the 1840s, was simultaneously nurturing a bumper crop of major American painters including Frank Duveneck and John Twachtman. Stephen Spielberg's cinematic vision of America is rooted in Ohio; media magnate Ted Turner has an equally keen feel for the nation's pulse. Astronauts John Glenn (now U.S. senator) and Neil Armstrong stargazed in Ohio skies. Mainstream Akron produced rock rebels Chrissie Hynde and Devo. James Thurber grew up in Columbus, where agriculture and sports usually trump literature, but his home is now a local shrine. Why have so many Ohioans become American icons? It could be that the state's own experience endows them with a sense of limitless possibility. 🏈

Farm Near Canal by August Biehle, 1935. *Private Collection*

OHIO

"Buckeye State"
17th State

Date of Statehood
MARCH 1, 1803

Capital
COLUMBUS

Bird
CARDINAL

Flower
RED CARNATION

Tree
BUCKEYE

Wildflower
WHITE TRILLIUM

Mineral
FLINT

Insect
LADYBIRD BEETLE

Ohio's symbols range from the tried-and-true (the cardinal, deer, and ladybug are favored by several states) to the truly unique. Two of the symbols share a history: the buckeye tree (*Aesculus glabra*) gets its name from Indians who thought its nut resembled the eye of the whitetail deer. The first "Buckeye" may have been Colonel Ebenezer Sproat, an 18th-century magistrate whom local Indians greeted as *hetuck*

Cardinal and scarlet carnation

(buckeye)—presumably a compliment. The scarlet carnation was adopted as the state flower in 1904 in memory of President William McKinley, who always wore one in his buttonhole. And the wild white trillium decorates Ohio's forests, which once covered the entire state. The state seal features a wheat sheaf, a bundle of arrows, and a row of hills (possibly Mount Logan) with a rising sun behind and a river (the Ohio or the Scioto) before. The black racer snake, called

"With God All Things Are Possible"

State motto

Two ladybugs. *Photo Mark Smith/Photo Researchers.* Below: White trillium (*Trillium grandiflorum*), the state flower. *Ohio Department of Tourism*

the "farmer's friend" because it eats destructive rodents, is native to all 88 Ohio counties. Flint, the state mineral since 1965, is abundant in the southern part of the state; Indians chipped it for knives, spear points, and arrowheads, and later settlers found it useful for flintlock guns and millstones. 🐞

Tomato juice, the official state beverage. Ohio ranks second among the states in growing tomatoes. *Photo Van Bucher/Photo Researchers*

Whence "Ohio"?

The state takes its name from the great river that forms its southern border and which Native Americans called *Oh-ee-yo*—an Iroquois word variously translated as "large," "deep," or "beautiful river." It was adopted by French explorers and traders, who left records of the "Riviere Oyo." The Anglicized pronunciation "O-hie-o" came later. Another variant was invented by novelist Herman Melville in his satirical fable *Mardi;* in a new land called Vivenza (America) there lay "a distant western valley called Hio-Hio."

"Beautiful Ohio"

I sailed away;
Wandered afar;
Crossed the mighty restless sea;
Looked for where I ought to be.
Cities so grand, mountains above,
Led to this land I love.

Chorus
Beautiful Ohio, where the golden grain
Dwarf the lovely flowers in the summer rain.
Cities rising high, silhouette the sky.
Freedom is supreme in this majestic land;
Mighty factories seem to hum in tune, so grand.
Beautiful Ohio, thy wonders are in view,
Land where my dreams all come true!

Music by Mary Earl, original words by Ballard MacDonald, special lyrics by Wilbert B. McBride. "Beautiful Ohio" became the state song in 1969. Ohio also has a state rock song: "Hang on Sloopy," composed by Celina-born guitarist Rick Derringer, first recorded by Dayton group the McCoys in 1965, and a favorite of the Ohio State University Marching Band.

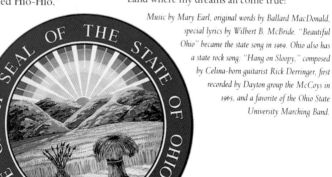

Eye of the Buck

Ohio alone claims the buckeye as its state tree and nickname. The Indians used their name for the tree, *Hetuck,* to refer to white settlers they admired. (So goes one story, although Indians also ground up the toxic nuts and scattered them on rivers to stun fish, making them easy to catch.) William Henry Harrison adopted the buckeye for his 1840 presidential campaign: to symbolize his rough-and-ready image, supporters carried buckeye canes and mounted a buckeye log cabin on wheels to stage a rally in Columbus. Soon everyone knew that Ohioans were "Buckeyes," and the success of Ohio State's teams spread the name's fame far and wide. Ohio's flag bears a red-and-white circle, said to represent a buckeye.

Buckeye Balls

These sweet confections resemble the inedible nut of the buckeye only in looks.

½ cup butter, melted
1 pound confectioner's sugar
1½ cups peanut butter
1 teaspoon vanilla extract
2 cups semisweet chocolate chips
1 tablespoon shortening

Combine melted butter, sugar, peanut butter, and vanilla; mix well. Refrigerate 1 hour or until firm. Roll into 1-inch balls and place on waxed paper. In top half of a double boiler melt chocolate chips and shortening, stirring constantly. Use a toothpick to dip balls into melted chocolate, leaving a small uncovered area so balls resemble buckeyes. Place balls on waxed paper. Blend in toothpick holes with fingers. Refrigerate until firm. Makes 3 dozen.

c. 100 B.C.–400 A.D. Hopewell Culture natives inhabit southern Ohio, building earthworks, trading widely.

1669 French explorer La Salle enters land between Lake Erie and the Ohio River.

1745 First British fort, Ft. Sandoski, completed on Sandusky Bay.

1761 First permanent dwelling built in Ohio, a log cabin near Bolivar.

1763 Ottowa chief Pontiac leads an Indian alliance against white settlers.

1773 Moravian mission opens first school west of the Alleghenies, at Schoenbrunn.

1783 Col. George Rogers Clark secures Ohio and surrounding territory for the new U.S.

1794 Gen. Anthony Wayne defeats Indian confederation at Battle of Fallen Timbers, ending 20 years of frontier war.

1796 Moses Cleaveland lays out a town site that becomes Cleveland. First book published in Ohio, *Maxwell's Code*, printed in Cincinnati.

1799 Territorial government established with capital at Cincinnati.

1800 Population in Territory of Ohio, 43,365. *Scioto Gazette,* state's oldest newspaper, begins publication at Chillicothe.

1801 John Chapman (Johnny Appleseed) plants orchard on banks of Licking Creek, near Etna.

1803 Ohio joins the Union as the 17th state.

1811 The *New Orleans,* first steamboat on western waters, travels down the Ohio.

1813 Oliver Hazard Perry defeats British fleet on Lake Erie.

1814 Oil and gas discovered while drilling for salt in Noble County.

1816 After several moves, state capital permanently established at Columbus.

1819 Thomas Cole begins painting at Steubenville.

1824 Kenyon College founded as Protestant Episcopal Theological Seminary.

1827 Cincinnati *Daily Gazette,* first daily newspaper in Midwest, begins publication.

1832 Ohio and Erie Canal, connecting Cleveland and Portsmouth, completed.

1833 Oberlin College founded.

1837 First abolitionist convention in U.S. held at Mount Pleasant.

1840 William Henry Harrison becomes first Ohio resident elected president.

1842 Charles Dickens tours Ohio recording comments on its people and life.

1857 Railroad Panic causes widespread unemployment and bank failures.

1860 Rookwood Pottery founded in Cincinnati.

1863 In Morgan's Raid, Confederate cavalry dash briefly into Ohio.

1868 Ulysses S. Grant of Ohio elected president.

1870 John D. Rockefeller organizes Standard Oil in Cleveland. Benjamin F. Goodrich begins manufacture of rubber goods in Akron.

1873 Painter Frank Duveneck returns to Cincinnati after studies in Munich.

1876 Ohioan Rutherford B. Hayes elected president. Archibald Willard's *Spirit of '76* exhibited at American Centennial Exposition.

1880 Ohioan James A. Garfield elected president.

1890 United Mine Workers union formed in Columbus.

1894 Paul Laurence Dunbar publishes first book of poetry at Dayton.

1896 William McKinley elected president after campaign managed by Cleveland boss Marc Hanna.

1900 Population 4,157,545.

1908 Ohioan William Howard Taft elected president.

1909 Leopold Stokowski becomes conductor of Cincinnati Symphony Orchestra.

1916 Cleveland Museum of Art opens.

1919 Sherwood Anderson publishes *Winesburg, Ohio.* Cincinnati Reds win World Series, later tainted by "Black Sox" scandal.

1920 Warren G. Harding becomes president. Cleveland Indians win World Series. American Professional Football Association formed in Canton.

1930 Terminal Tower Building opens.

1937 Most disastrous flooding ever occurs in Ohio River Valley, January.

1962 Ohioan John Glenn orbits the earth.

1967 Carl Stokes becomes the first African-American mayor of a major city (Cleveland).

1969 Ohioan Neil Armstrong becomes the first person to walk on the moon; oil slick on the Cuyahoga River catches fire.

1970 National Guard troops kills four students during an antiwar demonstration at Kent State University, sparking student strikes nationwide.

1974 Ohio's first national park, the Cuyahoga Valley National Recreation Area, created.

1995 Negotiations at Wright-Patterson Air Force Base near Dayton lead to the Bosnian peace agreement. Rock & Roll Hall of Fame and Museum opens in Cleveland.

1999 Jacobs Field, new Cleveland Indians' ballpark, opens.

2000 Population 11,256,654 (7th in nation).

2003 Ohio celebrates bicentennial of statehood.

Mill Creek Valley, Cincinnati **by Thomas Buchanan Read, n.d.** *Christie's Images*

"THESE ARE THE FIRST TIDINGS THAT HAVE EVER SOUNDED LIKE *FAME* to my ears—to be read on the banks of the Ohio!"

Lord Byron, on learning that his book Childe Harold *was in the Coonskin Library in the Ohio wilderness, c. 1815*

Ohio, the first state of the Midwest, unfolds gently westward from Appalachian hills into plains. Ice Age glaciers leveled the northern and western landscape, leaving fertile sediments behind; the glacier-free southeast tends to hills, ridges, and shaded valleys—farming came harder there. Northward the state is bounded by Lake Erie and the state of Michigan, while its serpentine southern border is drawn by the Ohio River. Mississippi-bound, the Ohio is fed by scores of tributary streams, including the Muskingum, the Scioto, and the Miami and Little Miami rivers. Other major rivers flow to the Great Lakes watershed: the Sandusky, the Cuyahoga, and the Maumee (which, after the Nile, is the world's longest northward-running river).

Ohio's geography made it easy to reach, easy to traverse, and equally suited to agriculture and industry. Thick forests covered most of the primeval state, but the settlers who cleared them found rich soils, beneath which lay equally rich deposits of coal, oil, gas, iron ore, clay, and limestone: the stuff of modern industry. After nearly two centuries of energetically exploiting its physical resources, Ohioans now look to restore some of their state's natural glory: for example, Lake Erie and the Cuyahoga River, once notoriously polluted, have seen massive environmental clean-ups. ✒

Banks of the Ohio

Ohio River Near Marietta by Henry Cheever Pratt, 1855. Marietta lies at the Ohio River's confluence with the Muskingum, not far from the West Virginia border. Christie's Images

The mighty, meandering Ohio River flows between the hills of Ohio on one bank, West Virginia and Kentucky on the other, and tends to unite those living on both banks. Southern Ohioans have more in common with their Kentucky brethren than with Clevelanders, say. Not wide but deep, the Ohio moves more cubic feet of water yearly than any other tributary of the Mississippi and is navigable for its entire 981-mile length. So ever since humans could paddle, it has been a key highway for traveling west into the continent's interior. Ohio's earliest towns grew up on the river: Marietta, the first permanent white settlement, was founded in 1788; Steubenville, Gallipolis, and Cincinnati soon followed. Flatboats carried settlers and cargo during a storied era in the early 19th century; freight barges and tourist steamboats still ply its waters.

Seventy percent of the state's rivers and streams empty into the Ohio, and seasonal flooding is a perennial worry, though the river system—including the Muskingum, the Miami, and other tributaries—has long since been tamed with dams and locks. Yet much of the Ohio valley, with its winding course and wooded flanking hills, remains picturesque, drawing hikers and sightseers today as it drew leading American landscapists a century ago.

"THE MAP AND THE HISTORY OF AMERICA REQUIRED THE westward-flowing Ohio."

Walter Havighurst, Ohio: A Bicentennial History, *1976*

The Great National Painting

After journeying up and down the Ohio four times, Samuel A. Hudson in 1848 unveiled his astounding "Great National Painting of the Ohio and Mississippi . . ." a panorama three-quarters of a mile long, executed on 20,000 feet of canvas and depicting 1,400 miles of river scenery. It drew crowds when shown in East Coast and European cities; the original was destroyed by fire.

Early fall along the Muskingum River near Dresden in Muskingum County. *Photo Ian Adams*

Plateau and Plain

A diagonal through southeastern Ohio marks the western end of Appalachia and the beginning of the Midwest. Topographically the state comprises three regions: the hilly Allegheny Plateau, the northerly Lake Plains, and the Central Plains in the west. Overall the theme is flatness: the highest point, Campbell Hill in Logan County, lies just 1,549 feet above sea level. Wetlands once flourished in the low-lying glaciated regions; the notorious Black Swamp covered a vast swath of northwestern Ohio until it was drained, yielding rich soil and natural gas deposits.

All of the plains terrain is hospitable to farming, with the many north-south-flowing rivers providing transport to market. Thus Ohio was a leading farm state through the mid-19th century, and its corn, livestock, and produce are still among the nation's best. The state is heavily developed now, but wild landscapes endure along river corridors, in patches of prairie, and in Ohio's Appalachia, where Wayne National Forest offers a haven for wildlife. Native fauna includes healthy populations of white-tailed deer, Canada geese, foxes, and pheasants; and the rare coyote, bobcat or bear. Weather-wise, Ohio is temperate with occasional extremes. Warm, moist air coming up the Mississippi valley often meets cold fronts moving south over Lake Erie to create violent storms; spring is the season for tornadoes and flooding.

"OUR POSITION IN THE NATION IS PECULIARLY felicitous, as to soil, climate, and productions, and it will be our own fault if we are not the happiest people in the Union."

Caleb Atwater, 1838

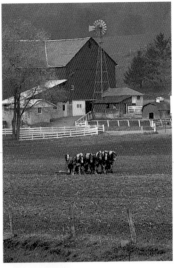

A horse-drawn plow on an Amish farm in Holmes County. *Photo Roger Bickel/New England Stock Photo.* Left: Sunrise in Richland County. *Photo Randall L. Schieber Opposite: U.S. Mail/ Brandywine Landscape* by William Sommer, 1938 (detail). *Collection of Joseph M. and Elsie Erdelac*

Put-in-Bay, Lake Erie.
Photo Randall L. Schieber
Below: The north shore
of Kelley's Island in Lake
Erie. Popular with vaca-
tioners, Kelley's Island
has a picturesque down-
town and, in Glacial
Grooves State Memorial,
some of the continent's
most dramatic evidence
of glacier travel. *Photo
Ian Adams*

Lake Erie's Shores

Lakefront forms two-thirds of Ohio's northern border—what Midwesterners have taken to calling the "North Coast." This is the state's flattest landscape, thanks to the glaciers, and some of its most fertile. Lake Erie itself is the shallowest of the Great Lakes and the smallest after Lake Ontario—57 miles wide at most and 210 feet deep at its profoundest. Its shores of glacial clay and boulders are lined with industrial cities (Ohio has eight Lake Erie ports), affluent suburbs, summer resorts, sheltered bays, and beaches. Several islands, also vacation destinations, lie on Ohio's side of the international boundary.

Its Great Lakes connection has shaped the state from the days of the voyageurs. Commerce on these

Lake Erie Cliff, Lakewood by William Sommer, 1911. In the mid-20th century, industrialization wreaked havoc with the lake's fisheries and recreation. But clean-up efforts have greatly improved matters, and Erie's shore remains Ohio's playground as well as a working coast. *Collection of Joseph M. and Elsie Erdelac*

shores began with the fur trade and expanded with canal link-ups to New York and the Ohio River in the early 1800s. Petroleum, coal, and steel production, and the need to transport raw materials and goods, created booming ports and industrial centers in Cleveland, Lorain, and Toledo.

"In all the world no trip like this!"

Slogan of a Great Lakes passenger ship company

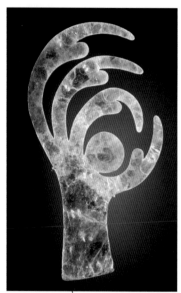

A bird's foot made out of mica, from the Hopewell Culture. *Ohio Historical Society. Photo Richard A. Cooke/Corbis*

First Peoples of Ohio

The land we know as Ohio has been inhabited since about 13,000 B.C. by successive groups of natives. Paleo-Indians, the earliest of these, hunted large game such as mammoths, bison, and deer using weapons made of flint from several Ohio sites—notably Flint Ridge in Licking County—until about 7000 B.C. The Archaic people (8000 to 500 B.C.) were somewhat less nomadic, burying their dead in glacial moraines, gathering nuts and shellfish. Next came several Woodland peoples, from about 800 B.C. to 1200 A.D. Best known are the Adena and Hopewell cultures, who built villages, cultivated crops, made pottery, and left ample evidence of their lives: earthworks, dwelling sites, and examples of decorative art. Archaeologists have excavated extensive villages and earthworks near Newark, Chillicothe, Marietta, and Portsmouth, including extraordinary effigy mounds such as the Great Serpent Mound in Adams County. Objects unearthed at these sites suggest that the Adena and Hopewell traded widely with other Indians as far away as the Rocky Mountains and Ontario for materials such as copper, silver, mica, and obsidian. Probably nowhere else north of Mexico did the decorative arts reach as high a plane as they did here during the Hopewell Culture (100 B.C. to 400 A.D.).

The Great Serpent Mound in Adams County. One theory is that it might have served as an astronomical calendar. *Photo Richard A. Cooke/Corbis*

"It is no exaggeration to state that that the entire person glittered with mica, pearl, shell and copper. All that the ancients could give him were showed upon his remains. . . . Perhaps a thousand beads, many of them pearl, were strewn about everywhere."

Archaeologist Warren K. Moorehead, describing his discovery of the remains of a high-ranking chief in the Hopewell Mounds

This 8-inch-tall man, made by the Adena, is the only carved pipe in human form among hundreds that have been found in prehistoric burial sites in the Ohio River Valley. *Ohio Historical Society*

Prehistoric Native Sites

Fort Ancient State Memorial
Near Lebanon, 513-289-2095
Displays span 15,000 years of Indian heritage on the site of a Hopewell bluff-top enclosure.

Great Serpent Mound
Adams County, 513-587-2796
Largest serpent effigy in North America, created around A.D. 1070; open April to mid-Nov.

Miamisburg Mound State Memorial
Outside Dayton; the state's largest Indian mound, with stairs to the top.

Newark Earthworks
Central Newark, 740-344-1919
Several ambitious earthworks from Hopewell period. The Moundbuilders State Memorial is nearby.

Flint Ridge State Memorial
Near Brownsville, 614-787-2476
Where prehistoric and historic Indians came to quarry flint for tools and weapons.

Traders and Warriors

In the historical era, Ohio's chief tribes were the Erie in the northeast; the Miami in the southwest; the Shawnee, ranging north across the Ohio; the Delaware in the southeast; and some Wyandot and Ottawa in the northwest. Warriors from the Iroquois nation raided westward periodically, keeping things unsettled. Like most Midwestern natives, those in Ohio became deeply involved in the fur trade and thus in the struggle among the French, English, and

A possible portrait of Tecumseh, the Shawnee Indian leader, by an unknown artist. *Chicago Natural History Museum* Right: Tecumseh's tomahawk. *Ohio Historical Society*

colonials to control North America's interior. Key figures included the Ottawa chieftain Pontiac, who tried to unite the western tribes in rebellion against British rule; Little Turtle of the Miami, who routed an American force in 1791; and the Shawnee leader Tecumseh, who joined the British in the War of 1812 in a last desperate fight to reclaim the Ohio Valley from America.

"THE AMERICAN FOREST NEVER PRODUCED A man more shrewd, politic, and ambitious."

Historian Francis Parkman on Pontiac

Prize of Empires

LaSalle was the first European to explore the Ohio River country, in 1669, and France claimed the land between the river and Lake Erie for its Great Lakes empire. While the French built forts, English traders from Pennsylvania and Virginia began venturing down the Ohio, and some settlers followed. The British too realized that the Ohio country was key to controlling the upper Mississippi valley, and both nations cultivated Indian allies in more than a century of striving for dominance. England prevailed in the colonial wars, but lost its prize to the new United States just a few years later. In the Revolutionary War, a young Kentuckian, Colonel George Rogers Clark, secured the Ohio country and the entire Northwest Territory for the Americans.

The Spirit of '76 by Archibald Willard, 1895.
Ohio Historical Society

"THE WINE, AS THEY DOSED THEMSELVES PRETTY PLENTIFULLY WITH IT, SOON BANISHED THE restraint which at first appeared in their conversation. . . . They told me that it was their absolute design, to take possession of the Ohio, and by G—d they would do it."

George Washington, on his negotiations with the French in 1752, to Virginia's Governor Dinwiddie

Ohio Fever

Settlers wasted no time in flocking to Ohio after the War of Independence. The older states had already staked claims: Connecticut's land grant included a strip of northeastern Ohio known as the Western Reserve, whose towns and architecture came to echo New England. Virginia military veterans were awarded lands north of the Ohio River, which took on a Tidewater flavor, while Pennsylvania Germans spread their culture through the central region. The Northwest Ordinance of 1787 defined borders, set requirements for statehood, and forbade slavery within the Northwest Territory; by 1803, Ohio settlers were numerous and well-organized enough to apply for statehood.

Earlier claimants didn't give up easily, however. The Shawnee and their allies made a stand in western Ohio, and President Washington needed to send his old comrade General "Mad Anthony" Wayne to defeat them at the Battle of

View of Cincinnati by J. C. Wild, mid-1830s. Wild was in Cincinnati during the years 1833–37 and made several watercolors of the city. Cincinnati Historical Society

"We have met the enemy and they are ours."

Commander Oliver Hazard Perry

The Battle of Lake Erie by William H. Powell, 1846. Commander Oliver Hazard Perry led the U.S. fleet in this pivotal victory in the War of 1812. *Ohio Historical Society Below:* An anonymous portrait of General Anthony Wayne, from the early 1800s. *Courtesy Henry Francis du Pont Winterthur Museum*

Fallen Timbers in 1791. Later, British loyalists in the west conspired to arm the Indians during the War of 1812. Future president William Henry Harrison invaded Michigan, and American sailors decisively defeated an English fleet in the Battle of Lake Erie. Settlement safely and swiftly proceeded—between 1800 and 1820, Ohio's population multiplied seven times; by 1850 it was the third most populous state.

"A SPIRIT OF EMIGRATION TO THE WESTERN COUNTRY IS VERY predominant. Congress has sold in the last year a pretty large quantity of lands in the Ohio for public securities, and thereby diminished the public debt considerably."

George Washington, in a letter to the Marquis de Lafayette, 1787

WAYNE

Freedom Train

A state in the middle, Ohio was pulled two ways as the Civil War approached. Abolitionist sentiment ran strong in the northern counties, with their New England heritage, whereas many in southern Ohio felt more kinship with the slave states across the river. Leaders of the antislavery movement included the Rev. Lyman Beecher, head of Lane Seminary in Cincinnati; Theodore Weld, who founded Oberlin College as America's first co-racial college; and Underground Railroad leader Levi Coffin. Cincinnati was a center of Railroad activity and the home of Harriet Beecher Stowe, whose *Uncle Tom's Cabin* dramatized a slave's escape across the Ohio River from Kentucky.

Ohio helped nominate and elect Lincoln and sent more than 300,000 Union soldiers to the battlefields. It also sent staunch Union leaders to Washington: Senator Salmon P. Chase, Secretary of War Edwin Stanton, Congressman Joshua

Giddings. Three great Union generals—Ulysses S. Grant, William Tecumseh Sherman, and Philip Sheridan—were Ohioans. Yet as the war dragged on, the Peace Democrats party—Copperheads to their foes—gained strength under their charismatic leader Clement L. Vallandigham. Exiled to the South, Vallandigham made his way to Canada and from there ran for Ohio governor in 1864, but he was soundly beaten by the Republican John Brough.

"FARMERS OF RICH AND JOYOUS OHIO, AND YE OF THE wide prairie states, answer—is this a thing for you to protect and countenance?"

Harriet Beecher Stowe, on the brutality of slavery, in Uncle Tom's Cabin, 1852

General Ulysses S. Grant in 1865.
Library of Congress

Civil War Sites

Harriet Beecher Stowe House
Walnut Hills, 513-632-5120
Stowe's father, Lyman Beecher, built this simple house and helped organize the Underground Railroad network.

Rankin House State Memorial
Ripley, 513-392-1627
1828 home of Rev. John Rankin, a major stop on the Underground Railroad.

Grant's Birthplace/Grant's Boyhood Home
Both outside Cincinnati, the former (513-553-4911) is a small frame house; the latter (513-378-4222) is more spacious.

Johnson's Island
Off Marblehead Peninsula on Lake Erie, 800-441-1271
Earthen forts mark the site of a POW camp for captured Confederates; also a Confederate cemetery.

From Ohio's Farms

Once settlers had cleared the forests, Ohio's river bottoms and plains began producing bounties of corn and other grains, orchard crops, and vegetables. Lack of transportation in the early days limited markets, so farmers found other ways to use crops: milling grain, distilling it into whiskey, and feeding it to livestock. Hog raising in the corn-rich southwest helped build Cincinnati, which was known as "Porkopolis" in the 1840s; the city's soap industry also began with hog byproducts. Mills sprang up on swift-flowing rivers, and Ohio's ground corn and flour were prized. Shipping by river, road, and canal helped make Ohio the leading farm state by 1850, but the western plains states soon overtook it.

Good Crop by Clarence Holbrook Carter, 1942. *The Schoen Collection, Miami. Right:* One-half million hogs were slaughtered in Ohio in 1848—this would make a string of sausages long enough to circle the globe twice. *Photo Herbert Schwind/Okapia/ Photo Researchers*

Farming, including poultry and eggs, remains important in much of the state. In Wayne County (Wooster) is the 2,000-acre Ohio Agricultural Research and Development Center, largest of its kind in the nation and site of the famed Secrest Arboretum. And why is tomato juice the state beverage? Because Ohio grows more tomatoes than any state except California.

An Amish farm near Berlin, Holmes County. Wayne, Holmes, and Tuscarora counties are home to the world's largest community of Amish farmers—visitors are welcomed at demonstration farms and villages offering hearty, homemade Amish food. *Photo Ian Adams. Below:* In an Ohio cornfield in the 1870s. *Cincinnati Historical Society*

"Down by the Old Mill Stream"

Down by the Old Mill Stream,
where I first met you,
with your eyes of blue,
dressed in gingham too,
It was there I knew,
that you loved me true,
You were sixteen,
my village queen,
by the old mill stream . . . .

Words and music by Tell Taylor, 1910. Taylor grew up in Hancock County near the old Mesamore Mill on Blanchard Creek.

Working on the Water

Ohio's waterways, natural and manmade, have always been the lifeblood of its commerce. Flatboats and keelboats (which could go upstream as well as down) were the first working craft on the Ohio River—bringing settlers in, shipping farm products out, moving passengers and goods between towns. The rough-and-ready keelboatman, epitomized by legendary Mike Fink, spawned many tall tales. The steamboat era began in 1811 when the *New Orleans* set out from Pittsburgh to the Gulf; at the peak of

Freighters by Carl Gaertner, 1931. *The Inlander Collection of Great Lakes Regional Painting. Below:* A boat on the Ohio River passes under the Brent Spence Bridge. Today, the Ohio carries more tonnage than the Panama Canal: oil, coal, grain, steel, and other bulk cargo travel the re-engineered river in giant barges pushed by towboats. *Photo Jim Schwabel/New England Stock Photo*

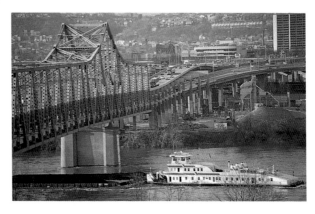

steamboat commerce in 1850, 740 of the stately craft plied the Ohio and the Mississippi. When railroads became more efficient than river travel in the late 1800s, Ohio shipyards began building steamboats for far off-rivers: the Nile, the Congo, and the Amazon.

The problem of getting inland harvests to the Ohio or Lake Erie inspired

Ohio's canal-building boom in the 1830s and 1840s. Soon a series of canals linked Cleveland with Portsmouth, Cincinnati with Dayton and eventually Toledo—and, via New York's Erie Canal, brought Ohio's crops all the way to the Atlantic. Land values near the canals soared; service industries sprang up along the towpaths. The canal era was relatively brief but helped grow the state in a hurry. In the 20th century, the focus of commerce shifted to Lake Erie, with its industrial ports and important fisheries. And since the St. Lawrence Seaway opened, big ships use Lake Erie for international trade.

Pioneers traveling down the Ohio River in a flatboat, in an undated color woodcut. *Corbis. Below: An unusual Dayton Canal scene, n.d. Ohio Historical Society*

HI-O, AWAY WE GO,
Floating down the river on the O-hi-o!

Keelboat song

The White Dam by Raphael Gleitsmann, n.d. *Christie's Images. Opposite top: Declarant* by Gerrit Beneker, 1919. *Private Collection, Laurie Platt Winfrey, Inc. Opposite bottom: Miners at work in New Straitsville. Ohio Historical Society*

With its abundant resources and fortunate geography, Ohio was destined to become an industrial powerhouse. Steel and rubber may come to mind first, but Ohio's industries have ranged from cars to ceramics, aircraft parts to pillows. Most have relied on the state's own raw materials—coal, oil, natural gas, sand, clay, and stone. Once a center of milling, meat-packing, and brewing, Cincinnati later produced agricultural machinery, machine tools, and soap products (Proctor & Gamble is there). Cleveland and other Lake Erie cities capitalized on their access to materials and became steel-making centers. A young John D. Rockefeller saw the advantages of kerosene over coal oil and organized the Standard Oil Company; within five years, pipelines and tank cars were carrying crude oil to his Cleveland refineries.

Toledo, next door to a huge natural gas field in the

Maumee Valley, used the cheap energy to fuel glass-making and other industries. Akron, once the world's capital for rubber goods, still has branches of Firestone, Goodyear, and B. F. Goodrich, though tires are mostly made elsewhere. The Wright Brothers of Dayton branched out from a bicycle shop to experiments in aviation, and a tiny Dayton company that made a "mechanical money drawer" grew into National Cash Register. Second only to Michigan in the early days of automobiles, Ohio is back in the car business with a new Honda plant in East Liberty. 🏈

"FREE FUEL! FREE LIGHTS! FREE SITES! FOR the Manufacturer Who Will Locate in Findlay, Ohio"

Hancock County Chamber of Commerce broadside

Art Deco screen, designed by Paul Fehrer of Rose Iron Works, Inc., 1930. Labor and capital inevitably clashed in Ohio's minefields and factories; from that long saga came progress for workers and noted labor leaders like the AFL's William Green. *The Rose Family Collection, Courtesy Cleveland Museum of Art*

Steel Cities

To make steel, you need iron ore, coal, and limestone—all within close reach of the Lake Erie ports. Iron ore was discovered in the Mahoning Valley in the early 1800s. But vaster sources of ore lay in the iron ranges ringing Lake Superior; limestone was plentiful around Lake Huron; and coal laced the hills of southern Ohio, Pennsylvania, and West Virginia. The Great Lakes became highways: in 1855 the first of countless ore ships from upper Michigan reached Cleveland. Advances in using coal as fuel for iron- and steel-making spurred on mining companies and manufacturers. Cleveland, Lorain, and Toledo became steel cities, as did the towns along the Mahoning, especially Youngstown. The new railroads, taking direct routes through the flat lake plains, further stimulated industrial growth.

"BY COMBINING COAL AND ORE IN A FURNACE AND ROASTING THEM together, men transmute iron through steel into gold."

Reporter for the Atlantic Monthly, *on the Ohio scene, 1899*

Fire and Ice

Industry and aesthetics met in Ohio's ceramics and glass-making traditions. Extensive deposits of fine molding clay in eastern and southern Ohio encouraged the creation of potteries in towns like

Newcomb College Pottery and Rookwood earthenware vases. *Christie's Images. Below:* A vase by Jacques Sicard for Weller Pottery, 1902. *Dayton Art Institute. Below left:* An important leaded glass "vine border" shade and ceramic and copper table lamp, from Rookwood and Tiffany. *Christie's Images*

Zanesville and East Liverpool, and wares produced in the early decades of the 20th century are highly collectible. Ohio's best-known potteries include Brush, McCoy, Roseville, and Weller, but the most renowned is Cincinnati's Rookwood Pottery, whose distinctive creations were acclaimed world-wide and are now prized by museums and collectors.

Glassmaking was begun in Toledo in the late 1880s by Edward Libbey and Michael Owens, and the city became the world's leading producer of industrial glass: bottles, chandeliers, auto and plate glass. Decorative glass had its place too, and locally made Art Deco glass tile adorns the Toledo Library. The excellent Toledo Public Art Museum has an outstanding collection of glass ancient and modern.

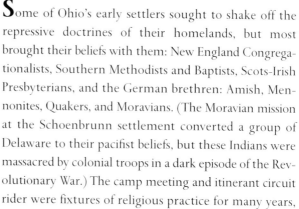

Kirtland Mormon Temple in Lake County. The Latter-Day Saints' first house of worship, the temple was built in 1833–36 according to scriptural instruction, from local sandstone and timbers. Combining Greek, Georgian, Gothic, and Federalist styles, it is a National Historical Landmark.
Photo Ian Adams

Some of Ohio's early settlers sought to shake off the repressive doctrines of their homelands, but most brought their beliefs with them: New England Congregationalists, Southern Methodists and Baptists, Scots-Irish Presbyterians, and the German brethren: Amish, Mennonites, Quakers, and Moravians. (The Moravian mission at the Schoenbrunn settlement converted a group of Delaware to their pacifist beliefs, but these Indians were massacred by colonial troops in a dark episode of the Revolutionary War.) The camp meeting and itinerant circuit rider were fixtures of religious practice for many years, and in frontier settlements the "emotional" sects often took hold: Holy Rollers, Jerkers, Laughers, and Dancers; Campbellites, Millerites, and more.

Ohio was the first step in the Latter-Day Saints' westward pilgrimage: Joseph Smith arrived at Kirtland in 1831 with a hundred or so followers and departed for Missouri a few years later with 25,000. Catholics and Jews were few until the late-19th-century migrations of eastern and southern Europeans, then became major presences in urban areas. Protestants are everywhere, and several denominations founded centers of

Amish children on their way to school in Holmes County. *Photo Jim Steinberg. Below:* Schoenbrunn State Memorial in New Philadelphia. *Photo Randall L. Schieber*

learning: Kenyon College (Episcopalian), Lane Theological Seminary (Presbyterian), and Western Reserve University (Congregationalist). Ohio's current cornucopia of faiths includes Southeast Asian Buddhists and Muslims—Toledo has a notable mosque. 🐖

"AS I WAS COMIN' ALONG TO MEETIN' I SAW A tree; I says to myself, Kin one man pull that ar tree up? No! Kin two men pull that ar tree up? No! . . . Kin twenty men pull that ar tree up? No! Kin God Almighty pull that tree up? Yes! I feel like suthin' is going to happen."

Parishioner Stoner, testifying at the Hardshell Baptist meetinghouse in Versailles, 1823

Safety Valve by Charles E. Burchfield, 1921. Burchfield was a pioneer in depicting what he called "the great epic poetry of midwest American life" and his personal connection to it, beginning in the 1920s. *Private Collection, Courtesy the Kennedy Galleries*

Getting Around

Lying in the path of national expansion, Ohio made efficient transportation an early priority: getting people to the state or through it on their way west, and shipping products out. Lake Erie and the Ohio River were easy routes of access, but traversing the interior was another matter. The brief but bustling canal era helped open up inland Ohio in the early 19th century; canal passengers could cross the state from lake to river in 80 hours. Around the same time, scores of Indian trails were being pounded into market roads, and the first major highway—the

National Road, now U.S. 40—was creeping its way from Cumberland, Maryland, across the West Virginia border, and through Columbus to the Indiana line, reached in 1838.

But rail soon trumped every other mode of transport. The first lines ran north and south, linking inland counties with the lake and river. Major east-west lines were completed in the 1850s: the Pittsburgh, Fort Wayne, and Chicago Railroad, the Marietta and Cincinnati in the south, and the Toledo, Norwalk and Cleveland skirting Lake Erie. During the peak railroad years, much of the nation's east-west transportation rolled through Ohio, and no other state had more miles of track in proportion to its area. Road-building never stopped, of course, and Ohio is crisscrossed with interstates, state highways, and backroads.

Riverboats lit at night along the Ohio River, in Columbus. Thousands of bridges, plain or picturesque, span rivers and streams. *Photo Roger Bickel/New England Stock Photo. Above:* A postcard of the High Level Bridge in Cleveland. *Ohio Historical Society*

The Iniswood Metro Gardens in Westerville. *Photo Randall L. Schieber* *Below:* Clifton Gorge in Hocking Hills State Park, near Logan. *Photo Randall L. Schieber*

Green Jewels

In its rush to industrialize, Ohio didn't neglect to set aside green spaces to refresh body and soul. All its major cities have cherished places such as Eden Park in Cincinnati and Columbus's Franklin Park. Cleveland's Metroparks manages 19,000 acres of parkland in 14 "reservations," where residents can golf or go fishing or rock climbing; public lands and beaches also dot the city's lakefront. Museums, zoos, conservatories, and other municipal treasures cluster in these big-city parks. Some have been touched by urban blight, but their value to city dwellers has never been clearer and funding their restoration has become a priority.

Around the countryside, 73 state parks offer recreation and camping on rivers and lakes, Lake Erie beaches, and in inland forests. Hocking Hills State Park, near Logan, is a highlight of the system with its caves, cliffs, waterfalls, and hemlock-shaded gorges. Wayne National Forest, an expanse of wild-lands bordering the Ohio River, draws thousands of hikers and naturalists. Northeast Ohio's natural jewel is the Cuyahoga Valley National Recreation Area: some 30,000 acres flanking the Cuyahoga River between Akron and Cleveland. The state's hard-working waterways have been much abused in the past, but Ohioans now recognize that clean rivers can enhance quality of life; a 50-mile "greenway" along the Little Miami River may be a model for future parks.

Lotus Lilies by Charles Courtney Curran, 1888, was painted at Lake Erie. *Terra Foundation of the Arts, Daniel J. Terra Collection*

Art in the Public Eye

Proud of their heritage and supportive of the arts, Ohioans have assembled a remarkable trove of artwork in public places. It would be hard to find a park, courthouse, or library that lacks a statue or memorial to Ohio's statesmen, servicemen, pioneers, or famous sons and daughters. Major museums in Cleveland, Cincinnati, and Toledo display works by prominent 20th-century sculptors including Henry Moore, Jacques Lipchitz, Louise Nevelson, Tony Smith, George Segal, and Anthony Caro. Noted contemporary artists such as Mark di Suvero, George Tsutakawa, Maya Lin, Isamu Noguchi, Jim Dine, and Nam June Paik have created commissioned works here.

Ohio's home-grown visions are often site-specific—David Evans Black's aluminum abstract *Flyover* in Dayton, saluting the Wright Brothers' experiments; Barry Gunderson's *Understorms* in the Franklin Park Conservatory of Columbus; or Gail

Topiary gardens by James T. Mason depicting Seurat's *A Sunday Afternoon on La Grande Jatte,* in Columbus. Photo Randall L. Schieber

A mural decorates a building in Marietta. *Photo Randall L. Schieber* Below: A sculptural fountain in Federal Building Plaza, in Cincinnati, headquarters of Proctor & Gamble. *Photo Kim Karpeles/Midwest Stock*

Larned's *King Corn* in the Department of Agriculture Building. Residents and visitors delight in whimsical pieces like James T. Mason's topiary rendition of Seurat's *A Sunday Afternoon on La Grande Jatte* in Columbus, or *Didy Wah Didy* by Billie Lawless, a vibrant billboard in metal, plastic, and neon near I-480 in Cleveland. Robert Dofford's quirky Floodwall Murals decorate 2,100 feet of concrete in Portsmouth. Much recent public art has been sponsored by the Ohio Arts Council's Percent for Art program. Another organization, The Sculpture Center in Cleveland, inventories and works to preserve outdoor sculpture in the state.

Temples of Learning

The people who settled Ohio were generally serious about getting on in life, and higher education was part of that mindset. From huge public universities to small liberal-arts colleges in picturesque towns, the educational spectrum is full. Ohio State University was founded as an Agricultural and Mechanical College in 1873; today nearly 50,000 students throng its Columbus campus, and Buckeye sports teams provoke annual mania in undergrads and alums. Akron's Kent State University, another premier public university, is known for its research programs (the liquid crystal display was invented here); a museum that features costumes, textiles, and glass; and its highly rated school of fashion design. Kent State's Center for Peaceful Change

Memorial Arch at Oberlin College. *Photo Jim Baron/Images Finders Right:* **The Conservatory of Music at Oberlin.** *Photo Randall L. Schieber*

serves as a living memorial to students killed or wounded during a May 1970 demonstration.

For a fairly conservative state, Ohio has fostered experimental, even radical, education. Oberlin College, founded in 1833, was the nation's first coed college and among the first to admit black students. A wellspring of the arts, it has a renowned music conservatory, and the Oberlin Dance Theater was formed here. Education pioneer Horace Mann established a nonsectarian, humanist tradition at Antioch College in Yellow Springs; later, the school developed innovative work-study methods. Case Western Reserve University is a leading research institution and cultural magnet in Cleveland. And classic small-town college life thrives in places like historic Kenyon College in Gambier, with its Charles Bulfinch–designed buildings, and Oxford's Miami University.

A memorial to the students slain at Kent State. *Photo Jim Baron/ Images Finders. Left:* Hall Auditorium stands amid fall foliage at Miami University in Oxford, which Robert Frost once called "America's prettiest campus." *Photo William A. Holmes/Images Finders*

"BE ASHAMED TO DIE UNTIL you have won some victory for humanity."

Horace Mann, first president of Antioch College, in his farewell speech to students

In 1998, Sen. John Glenn, the first American to orbit the earth, returned to space.
Agence France Presse/ Corbis-Bettmann

All of Ohio's native-born presidents were Republicans, and the state has mostly gone G.O.P. in national elections—but that's not the whole story. From 1854 to the 1940s, while giving its electoral votes to every Republican presidential candidate except Wilson and Roosevelt, Ohio elected 12 Democratic governors. Often the governor and legislative majorities come from opposing parties, making for lively clashes in Columbus. Ohio also is infamous for President Warren Harding's "Ohio Gang," the corrupt cronies who soiled his administration's record, and for two turn-of-the-century city bosses: Marcus A. Hanna of Cleveland and George B. Cox of Cincinnati. In contrast stand two reformers: Tom Johnson, who broke Hanna's hold on Cleveland, and Samuel (known as "Golden Rule") Jones, an oilman who became mayor of Toledo.

Distinguished Ohio statesmen of more recent vintage reflect the state's changing ethnic mix. They include five-term Democratic governor (and later senator) Frank Lausche; Anthony Celebrezze, who became mayor of Cleveland and secretary of health, education, and welfare in JFK's administration; Carl Stokes, the nation's first big-city black mayor (Cleveland); and multi-term Senator John Glenn. Current Governor Bob Taft is the scion of a great Ohio political family. His father and grandfather were U.S. senators; his great-grandfather was William Howard Taft, 27th president and Chief Justice of the Supreme Court (1921–30). 🖋

Carl Stokes in 1967, the night he won the election to become mayor of Cleveland. *Bettman/ Corbis. Below:* A cartoon of Boss Hanna, printed in *The Verdict,* November 13, 1889

"He found us groping leaderless and blind

He left the city with a civic mind"

Inscription on the Tom L. Johnson monument in Cleveland, 1915

President Warren Harding sits for his portrait bust, sculpted by Louis Keila, at his home in Marion. *Corbis. Opposite: These Are My Jewels* by Levi Tucker Schofield, 1894, features native sons Grant, Garfield, Hayes, Sherman, Sheridan, and Chase. The sculpture stands in Capitol Square, Columbus. *Ohio Historical Society*

Presidential Timber

When Will Rogers toured Japan, he was told that "O-hi-o" meant a friendly greeting—to which he responded, "Where I come from, it means 'president.'" Eight Ohioans have occupied the White House, more than any other state can boast. William Henry Harrison, a general in the War of 1812 and elected president in 1840, was born in Virginia but lived in North Bend, Ohio, most of his life. Civil War hero Ulysses S. Grant grew up in rural southern Ohio, though he was elected in 1868 while living in Illinois. (Among his opponents was the first woman presidential candidate, Victoria Woodhull, also an Ohioan.) Rutherford B. Hayes of Fremont, president from 1877–81, was a dyed-in-the-wool Buckeye, a Kenyon College graduate and three-term governor.

James A. Garfield, born near Cleveland, once drove a mule on the Ohio Canal, served in Congress, and was the "dark horse" Republican nominee in 1880; he was assassinated just five months after his election. Benjamin Harrison (grandson of Wm. Henry and also from North Bend), actually ran for president from Indiana.

Another Ohio governor, William McKinley, won White House terms in 1896 and 1900, upheld the gold standard, pursued the Spanish-American War, and also died by an assassin's hand. The aristocratic William H. Taft was Teddy Roosevelt's hand-picked successor in 1908. Last and most colorful, Warren G. Harding, elected in 1920, died in office surrounded by scandal. Theories abound as to why Ohio soil grew so much presidential timber; the prevailing one holds that Ohio stands for moderation and patriotic service in the nation's mind.

"WILL HAYS TOOK ME in to meet President Harding. I said 'Mr. President, I would like to tell you all the latest political jokes.' He said 'You don't have to, Will. I appointed them.'"

Will Rogers, How We Elect Our Presidents, *1952*

Presidential Places

James A. Garfield NHS
Mentor, 216-255-8722
Garfield's 30-room home, Lawnfield, now holds furnishings, memorabilia, and a library.

McKinley National Memorial and Museum
Canton, 330-455-7043
Neoclassical mausoleum of McKinley and his family; the adjacent museum houses memorabilia.

William Howard Taft NHS
Cincinnati, 513-684-3262
Mount Auburn birthplace of the 27th president.

Warren G. Harding Home and Museum, Harding Memorial
Marion, 614-387-9630
Harding ran his "front porch campaign" here; memorial is an imposing ring of classical columns.

At Home in Ohio

Ohio dwellings represent virtually every building style found in eastern America. Log cabins, used here much more than in the coastal states, were the earliest non-Indian homes, and authentic replicas can be seen at the reconstructed Moravian settlement at Schoenbrunn. Once established, settlers from different regions reproduced their typical architectural forms: New England colonials and Cape Cods, quasi-plantation houses in the Virginia Military District around Chillicothe, heavy stone farmhouses and barns in the central farmlands settled by German and Dutch families. A few late Georgian or Federal style houses appeared in the early 19th century; the finest is Taft House (now a museum) in Cincinnati.

By the 1840s, Greek Revival was the favored style for new homes, and many fine examples endure—followed soon by Gothic Revival and the whole gamut of Victorian and post-Victorian variations: Queen Anne, Tudor, Italianate,

French Eclectic, Romanesque. Many small towns, especially in the Western Reserve and southern Ohio, have successfully preserved and restored their historic homes; these include Wellington, Findlay, Mount Vernon, Piqua, and Marietta. The German Village in Columbus is another place to walk through history, with a distinct ethnic flavor. Ohio has its share, too, of fine modernist and contemporary homes, especially in the affluent suburbs. Most of the half-dozen Frank Lloyd Wright homes are private, but the Weltzheimer-Johnson Home in Oberlin, one of Wright's Usonian experiments, is open to visitors.

A Georgian Federal home built in 1832, in Lancaster. *Photo Roger Bickel/New England Stock Photo. Below: A Summer Day by James Weber, c. 1915. Private Collection, Courtesy Keny Galleries, Columbus. Opposite:* An 1855 Gothic Revival Castle in Marietta. *Photo Layne Kennedy/Corbis*

Great Estates

Mount Healthy, Ohio by Robert Scott Duncanson, 1844. National Museum of American Art, Smithsonian Institution, Washington, D.C./Art Resource

Ohio's industrialists and shipping tycoons spent their fortunes on Gilded Age palaces and country estates. In the late 19th century Cleveland's Euclid Avenue was a parade of English manor houses, French châteaux, and Italian palazzos, their interiors holding treasures from all corners of the earth. On the city's outskirts—and those of Cincinnati and Akron as well—the wealthy found more real estate to indulge their whims.

Gwinn, the home of Cleveland iron ore magnate William

Mather, is a serene Palladian villa on Lake Erie, designed by Charles Platt and set amidst notable gardens. Winding Creek Farm, featuring a gabled limestone manor house, was the 1,600-acre playground of Julius and Dorette Fleischmann in the exclusive Carmargo development outside Cincinnati. Massillon is proud of its Victorian Romanesque Five

Oaks Mansion, built in 1892–94 for the J. Walter McClymonds family, who later gave it to the Massillon Women's Club. And

on Akron's Portage Path is Stan Hywet ("stone quarry" in Old English), built by Goodyear co-founder Frank A. Sieberling. One of the Midwest's landmark estates, it has a Tudor Revival brick mansion, renowned landscape design by Warren Manning, and the nation's only restored Ellen Biddle Shipman garden open to the public.

The Tudor Revival brick mansion Stan Hywet, the Akron estate of Frank A. Sieberling, co-founder of Goodyear. *Photo Randall L. Schieber Left:* Peonies in the English garden, designed by Ellen Biddle Shipman, at Stan Hywet Hall. *Photo Ian Adams*

Azaleas in the Cleveland Botanical Gardens. *Photo Randall L. Schieber* Below: Tulips and other spring flowers cover the grounds at Gardenview Horticultural Park in Strongsville, in northeast Ohio. *Photo Ian Adams*

Ohio in Bloom

Even if most Ohioans today aren't farmers, the state's rich earth, generous growing season, and ample rainfall yield great rewards for horticulturists. Next best is visiting someone else's garden, and garden clubs around the state offer tours of outstanding private gardens. Public gardens and arboreta are found in nearly every part of Ohio. In Cleveland, the Cleveland Botanical Garden features Japanese, herb, rose, and knot gardens and a noted horticultural library; the Western Reserve Herb Garden is the second largest of its kind in the nation; and Rockefeller Park Greenhouses offers a unique talking garden for the blind. Cincinnati's Irwin Krohn Conservatory is a rainforest under glass, growing 5,000 species of rare tropical and desert plants, and Mt. Airy Arboretum specializes in landscaping with trees.

Holden Arboreteum in Lake County, at 3,100 acres, is the largest in the U.S. and among the most varied; natives make sure to come in all seasons, but spring's rhododendrons and azaleas are hard to top. Secrest Arboretum and the Garden of Roses of Legend and Romance are part of the Ohio Agricultural Research and Development Center in Wooster. On the Ohio University campus, the Wolfe Garden is shaped like the state; at Kingwood Center in Mansfield 40,000 tulips bloom each spring. The Glasshouse Works Greenhouses in Stewart, near Marietta, propagates and sells some of the world's rarest plants, drawing plant fanciers worldwide.

Sewing in the Garden by Yeteve Smith, c. 1915. *Private Collection, Courtesy Keny Galleries, Columbus*

State Fare and Fests

If not a mecca for sophisticated cuisine, Ohio won't let you go hungry. Hearty ethnic fare is the theme in most cities. Cleveland has strong Polish, Brazilian, Asian, and Italian traditions, and its historic West Side Market is an indoor/outdoor landmark with vendors of at least 20 nationalities. Hungarian and Greek pastries, corned beef, and Lake Erie walleye and perch are other local specialties. In Columbus you'll find German, Greek, and Spanish restaurants; Cincinnati is famed for chili and barbecue. Toledo boasts Tony Packo's restaurant—a destination since Radar on TV's *M*A*S*H* waxed nostalgic about its Hungarian hot dogs. Simple homemade fare reigns in rural areas, especially in Amish country, where menus often feature noodles, pot roast, locally made cheese, and peanut-butter pie. Breweries and brewpubs are also big in Ohio.

Ohio has more outdoor festivals than there are days of the

Pumpkins at the Circleville Pumpkin Fest. Fresh local vegetables and fruit are sublime when in season. *Photo Randall L. Schieber*

year, and many center on food. The Big Pig Gig in Cincinnati celebrates the city's heritage of raising and processing the noble porker; Oktoberfest in Columbus's German Village is a major event. Berea annually hosts the National Rib Cookoff, Bucyrus holds a Bratwurst Festival, and Obetz turns out in August for Zucchinifest. The Ohio Sauerkraut Festival takes place in Waynesville, and Vintage Ohio in Lake County showcases more than two dozen Buckeye wineries—Ohio ranks fifth among wine-producing states.

An Asian festival in Columbus. *Photo Randall L. Schieber. Left:* A German band plays at the Ohio Sauerkraut Festival in Waynesville. *Photo Randall L. Schieber*

Pete Rose by Andy Warhol, 1985. © *Estate of Andy Warhol/ARS, N.Y. Butler Museum of American Art, Youngstown* Right: **Cincinnati Reds star Ken Griffey, Jr., hits a 3-run homer against the Cleveland Indians, in June 2000.** *Photo Ron Kuntz, Reuters NewMedia, Inc./Corbis*

Taking the Field

Ohioans are devoted to their sports teams and have plenty to root for. Baseball historically ranks first, and Ohio's two major league squads own proud traditions. One of four charter members of the American League, the Cleveland Indians are the latest of many professional ball clubs to call the city home; baseball began here when the Cleveland Forest Citys took on the Cincinnati Red Stockings on June 2, 1869. The Cleveland Buckeyes were champions of the Negro League in 1945. The 1920 and 1948 Indians won World Series titles, and the team sent Tris Speaker, Satchel Paige, Bob Feller, Cy Young, and Ralph Kiner to the Hall of Fame. The Indians have contended for the pennant over much of the last decade, winning their division in 1999, and draw sellout crowds to cozy new Jacobs Field.

The national pastime is even older in Cincinnati: an amateur team, the Resolutes, was formed in 1866. In the first professional game ever (June 1, 1869), the Red

Minor League by Clyde Singer, 1946. Born in Malvern, Ohio, in 1908, Singer studied at the Columbus Art School and at the Art Students League in New York, where his teachers included Thomas Hart Benton and John Steuart Curry. He returned to Malvern to set up his studio, and in 1940 he began teaching at the Butler Institute of American Art. *Butler Museum of American Art, Youngstown*

Stockings beat the Mansfield Independents. The Reds won the Series in 1919 (the Series clouded by the infamous Black Sox scandal) and 1940, and in the starry 1970s, the Big Red Machine led by Pete Rose, Johnny Bench, Tony Perez, and Ken Griffey won four National League pennants and two World Series, setting countless records in the process. Rose was later kicked out of baseball for gambling but remains a hometown icon. Superstar outfielder Ken Griffey, Jr. returned to play for his hometown in 2000. Not to be outdone by their northern neighbors, the Reds in 2003 will relocate to a new ballpark overlooking the Ohio River. Minor-league teams with strong followings include the Columbus Clippers, the Chillicothe Paints (Sherwin-Williams is based here), and the Toledo Mud Hens!

On the Gridiron, Off the Boards

Pro football and basketball also have colorful histories in Ohio. Cincinnati had National Football League teams in the 1930s and 1940s— the Celts and the Bengals—then went teamless for nearly 30 years until the city was awarded an AFL expansion franchise in 1967. These latter-day Bengals went to the Superbowl in 1981 and 1988, but lost to San Francisco both times. The Cleveland Browns joined the All-American Football Conference in 1946 and dominated it for a decade. Jim Brown and Leroy Kelley were among the great players of the 1960s. After mostly losing seasons in the 1990s, owner Art Modell earned hisses by moving the franchise to Baltimore—but the team nickname and colors stayed in Cleveland, and the faithful "Dawgs" (as fans are known) were rewarded in 1999 with a new expansion team to carry on the legend. The Professional Football Hall of Fame is a year-round attraction in Canton.

The new Cleveland Browns, an expansion team, make a grand entrance onto the field of their stadium. *Photo David Maxwell, AFP Photo/Corbis*

Cleveland also has its basketball Cavaliers, a 30-year-old team with a great fan base but a middling record. Their best seasons, in the early '90s, coincided with Michael Jordan's NBA dominance, the Bulls knocking the Cavs out of the playoffs several times.

Go, Buckeyes!

Pro sports may grab the headlines, but Ohio fans' true passion is reserved for their OSU Buckeyes. Ohio State's football and basketball programs are extraordinarily successful, well supported, and tradition rich; in 1890, the school defeated Ohio Wes-

The OSU football band. *Images Finders. Below:* **Women's basketball at OSU.** *Wagner Photo/ Images Finders*

leyan in the first gridiron contest played in the state. Over the years Buckeye teams have won 9 national and 27 Big Ten championships, played in 29 bowl games (including 13 Rose Bowls), and fielded 145 All-Americans. OSU tailback Archie Griffin is the only two-time winner of the Heisman Trophy; current running back Eddie George was Ohio State's sixth Heisman winner. Buckeye basketball tournaments draw spectators from all over the state, and only Purdue and Indiana have won more Big Ten Championships. NBA greats Jerry Lucas and John Havlicek, among others, were OSU basketballers. These days, women's basketball is catching up to the men's program as a fan favorite. Of course, not every Ohioan is a sports fanatic—the outstanding exception is Columbus native and OSU graduate James Thurber, who delightfully skewered Buckeye "football jocks" in his 1940 Broadway hit, *The Male Animal.*

Fairest of the Fairways

Ohio's lush, gently rolling landscape was made to order for golf, probably its most popular individual pastime. In sheer numbers, the state ranks fifth nationally with 616 public and resort courses, and its outstanding private courses host major tour-

Golf tournament in Akron. *Photo Tony Roberts/Corbis. Below: Jack Nicklaus displays his PGA trophy in 1973, in Cleveland. Corbis*

naments. *Golf Digest*'s list of the best 100 courses in the U.S. includes Muirfield Village Golf Club in Dublin, The Golf Club in New Albany, Inverness Club in Toledo, Scioto Country Club in Columbus, and the Double Eagle Club in Galena, among others. Firestone Country Club in Akron, designed by Bertie Way and redesigned by Robert Trent Jones, is home of the World Series of Golf. Highly rated public courses include Foxfire Golf Club in Lockbourne and StoneWater in Highland Heights. Ohio native Jack Nicklaus is something of a state deity; his amazing career encompasses 70 PGA tour championships and more PGA and Masters victories than anyone else. The "Golden Bear" also designed several courses here.

Downhill Racers

Since 1935, Akron has hosted what some call the world's greatest amateur racing event: the All-American Soap Box Derby. The idea actually was born in Dayton, where news photographer Myron E. ("Scottie") Scott encountered three boys racing homemade, engineless cars down an inclined brick street and thought, why not a coasting race? Thus was born an event that would capture the imagination of Depression America and later draw entrants from around the world. In 1936, the WPA built an official Derby Downs complex, still in use with subsequent improvements. Derby fans have ranged from Eddie Rickenbacker and Tom Mix to General Jimmy Doolittle and actor Jimmy Stewart. Boys (and now girls) who have won local races come to run heats and, if lucky, make it to the finals. A former highlight of Derby week was the promotional Oil Can Trophy Race, in which celebrities raced in special oversized cars. In 1951, Ronald Reagan came in second to ventriloquist Paul Winchell and his dummy Jerry Mahoney.

Contestants cross the finish line in 1936. *Corbis. Below:* The All-American Soap Box Derby in Akron. *Photo Mark C. Burnett/ Photo Researchers*

Serious Summer Fun

The roller coaster at Paramount's Kings Island amusement park, near Cincinnati. *Photo Randall L. Schieber*
Opposite: A ride at the Ohio State Fair in Columbus. *Photo Randall L. Schieber*

When trader George Croghan landed in 1760 at Cedar Point—the tip of a narrow peninsula at the entrance to Sandusky Bay—it was a timbered wilderness where Ottawas and Wyandot camped. But its wide sandy beach made it a resort destination for Cleveland as early as the 1880s. At one time or another Cedar Point has featured dance halls, a skating rink, boating lagoons, and a miniature railroad line. Today three resort hotels, a marina, and an RV campground accommodate visitors to the country's largest theme park, where a new roller coaster called Millennium Force hurls riders at speeds up to 92 mph. Vintage carousels are a reminder of Cedar Point's past. Other large theme parks in northern Ohio are

Six Flags Ohio in Aurora and SeaWorld Cleveland Adventure Park. Near Cincinnati are Paramount's Kings Island; Coney Island, with its 200- by-400-foot pool; and The Beach Waterpark, named one of the country's top five waterparks.

Since 1850, the Ohio State Fair has been among the nation's premier agricultural fairs. Today many come to the Fairgrounds in Columbus for the rides or the big-name entertainment, but if you prefer livestock exhibits, prize-winning produce, harness racing, milking or quilting contests, you won't be disappointed. Fair traditions include the Butter Sculpture—since the early 1900s, a cow and calf have been carved from 1,500 pounds of butter—and events celebrating the llama, including the Llama Drill Team and Leaping Llamas obstacle course. Fair trivia: since 1948, visitors to the "Guess your age/weight booth" have guessed more than one billion pounds of weight—equal to 105,263 elephants.

Merry-Go-Round by **Clarence Holbrook Carter,** 1949. *Southern Ohio Museum, Portsmouth*

"ANYTHING ON A STICK IS OFFICIAL FAIR FOOD. How about cheese fries on a stick? It would make it much easier to carry. Or a funnel cake on a stick."

Posted by Ann Wright, from Whitehall, on the Ohio State Fair Memory Wall online

Sherwood Anderson was born in Camden, a quiet farming town near Dayton, in 1876; his family moved to Clyde in northern Ohio when he was four. Clyde is said to be the model for the town depicted in *Winesburg, Ohio.* Culver Pictures

Literary Ohio

No major literary movements have yet sprung from Ohio, and the state's noted writers conform to no pattern. Early literacy in the state was greatly advanced by William Holmes McGuffey, whose "McGuffey Readers" taught millions of young Americans to read. Sherwood Anderson saw northern Ohio change from the rural paradise of his boyhood to a hive of industry, and sounded a note of skepticism in his famed *Winesburg, Ohio* (1919). Zane Grey grew up in southern Ohio before heading west to write his rousing frontier tales; the National Road–Zane Grey Museum houses memorabilia. Strong African-American voices of two generations were formed in Ohio: poet Paul Laurence Dunbar and Nobel Laureate novelist Toni Morrison, whose *Beloved* is set outside Cincinnati. William Dean Howells, long-time editor of the *Atlantic Monthly,* was an Ohioan, as was the lyrical poet Hart Crane. Two recent Ohio novelists offer a contrast: the genre-bending satirist Thomas Berger, best-known for his *Little Big Man;* and Helen Hoover Santmyer, who gently dissects small-town life in *Ohio Town.* A unique Ohio presence was Louis Bromfield, who left a double legacy: his Pulitzer Prize–winning fiction (*Early Autumn,* 1926) and his Malabar Farm in Richland County, where he practiced conservation and entertained America's literary and show-business elite.

But the state's most beloved writer, archetypal in his oddness, was James Thurber. In his prose and drawings, Thurber, born and raised in Columbus, poked fun at its provincialism and found rich humor in its ordinary lives. Both *The Secret Life of Walter Mitty* and *Fables for Our Time* drew on his early experience. The Thurber house is now a literary center that hosts visitors, readings, and writers in residence.

"HALF MY BOOKS COULD NOT HAVE BEEN WRITTEN IF IT had not been for the city of my birth."

James Thurber, in Ohio Authors

"IN OHIO SEASONS ARE THEATRICAL. EACH ONE ENTERS like a prima donna, convinced its performance is the reason the world has people in it."

Toni Morrison, Beloved, 1987

Paul Laurence Dunbar, born and raised in Dayton, was the first African-American poet whose work was read by a wide audience. *Culver Pictures. Below:* Louis Bromfield at Malabar Farm. *Ohio Department of Tourism*

Ohio on Stage and Screen

Theater came to early Ohio with the occasional troupe of traveling players, in tent shows, and on Ohio River showboats. Around the turn of the century many towns built "opera houses" to showcase live performance. The movie steamroller suppressed theater activity for a time, but it was revived in the 1930s in Cleveland and Cincinnati by the Federal Theater Project. Today there are excellent regional companies around the state.

Jerry Mathers played the Beaver and Tony Dow was his big brother Wally on *Leave It to Beaver*. Photofest
Opposite: Drew Carey. Photofest

Historical drama thrives in the *Blue Jacket* outdoor drama in Dayton, the Shawnee saga *Tecumseh!* in Chilicothe, and *Trumpet in the Land,* a reenactment of the Moravian pioneers in New Philadelphia.

A remarkable array of stage and screen stars were Ohio natives, though their careers took them elsewhere. A short list would include Theda Bara, Dorothy Dandridge, Doris Day, Clark Gable, Dorothy and Lillian Gish, Joel Grey, Bob Hope, Dean Martin, Burgess Meredith, Paul Newman, Tyrone Power, and Roy Rogers. Films set in Ohio range from *The Man Who Came to Dinner* to *Major League*. The state also has provided All-American locales for TV shows such as *Leave It to Beaver, Mary Hartman, Mary Hartman* (set in fictional Fernwood), *WKRP in Cincinnati, Family Ties,* and *The Drew Carey Show.*

Reel-Life Ohio

Films with Buckeye State plot lines or settings include:

The Man Who Came to Dinner (1942)

A curmudgeon disrupts life in the home of a prominent but eccentric Ohio family. Monty Woolley heads a great cast.

Bye, Bye, Birdie (1963)

An Elvis Presley clone provokes teen hysteria in Sweet Apple, Ohio, in this madcap musical starring Ann-Margret.

The Rocky Horror Picture Show (1975)

Newlyweds Brad and Janet drive away from Denton, Ohio, but get lost in the rain. Tim Curry as Dr. Frank N. Furter leads the midnight madness.

American Hot Wax (1978)

True story of Cleveland disc jockey Alan Freed, who introduced teen radio audiences to rock'n'roll in the early 1950s.

Major League (1989)

A bunch of misfits make a run at the American League title; with Charlie Sheen.

Beloved (1998)

Film version of Toni Morrison's novel about former slaves after the Civil War.

Humming Along

The Mills Brothers, c. 1945. Originally a quartet of brothers from Piqua, Ohio, the Mills Brothers were a popular touring act for nearly 50 years beginning in the 1930s. *Corbis*

Ohio has lively traditions across the musical spectrum from classical to rock. The Cleveland Orchestra, founded in 1918, has attained high rank among symphonic orchestras worldwide. Maestro George Szell guided the orchestra to fame from 1946 to 1970; its other great conductors have included Erich Leinsdorf, Pierre Boulez, and Lorin Maazel. Current musical director Christoph von Dohnányi will be succeeded in 2002 by Franz Welser-Möst. Graceful Severance Hall, the orchestra's home since 1931, sparkles after a recent full-scale renovation. The Cincinnati Opera is a fine medium-size company, and Columbus, Toledo, Dayton, and Akron all support local symphonies, choruses, and opera troupes. Music conservatories at Baldwin-Wallace and Oberlin col-

Tin Pan Ohio

The Ohioana Library's Ohio Song Collection boasts more than 100 titles, including these:

"Don't Forget that You're a Buckeye"
by Nettie Butts McIntyre (1927)
'Mid the green fields of Ohio, the state where I was born . . .

"Ohio Is America, Too"
by G. R. Woodford and Edna Evelyn Geist (1943)
See Rome and die is an old- time refrain, but see Ohio and live again . .

"Round on the End and High in the Middle: O-H-I-O"
by Alfred Bryan and Bert Hanlon (1922)
Old man Biddle gave me a riddle, just the other day . . .

"When Erie's Wave Shall in Ohio Lave"
by John Playford and James S. Freeman (1825)
Hail! Hail! th' auspicious day

and of course **"Ohio"**
by Neil Young (1970)
Tin soldiers and Nixon's coming . . .

leges have spun off professional performing groups such as the Ohio Chamber Orchestra.

Popular songwriters and singers have flourished here since Stephen Foster worked as a bookkeeper on the Cincinnati waterfront in the 1840s, spinning out tunes like "Oh! Susanna" about the westward-faring riverboat passengers. Jazz tunesmith Billy Strayhorn was a Buckeye, as was composer/arranger Henry Mancini. Popular vocalists from Ohio include Kaye Ballard, Anita Baker, Sammy Kaye, the Mills Brothers, and Nancy Wilson. Music has its pantheons here, too: the American Classical Music Hall of Fame & Museum is in Cincinnati; the Polka Hall of Fame is near Cleveland.

"WHY, O WHY, O WHY O, WHY DID I EVER LEAVE OHIO?"
Lyric from "Ohio," from Bernstein, Comden and Green's Wonderful Town, *1953*

The Rock and Roll Hall of Fame and Museum designed by I. M. Pei, in Cleveland, has been one of the nation's top tourist draws since it opened in 1995. *Photo Randall L. Schieber*

Ohio Rocks

Some trace the birth of rock and roll to July 11, 1951, when disc jockey Alan ("Moondog") Freed at WXEL in Cleveland went on the air with the first radio show to program rhythm and blues for a white teenage audience. Freed coined the term "rock 'n' roll" to get around prejudice toward black music, and he helped unleash a sound that would change world culture. Cincinnati played its part, too: King Records was a force in R&B and rock and roll in the 1940s and '50s, its artists including the Platters, Hank Ballard and the Midnighters (who first recorded "The Twist"), and James Brown. Ohio performers range from Chrissie Hynde of the Pretenders (one song mourns the malling of her home state: "Where'd you go, Ohio?") to singer-songwriter Tracy Chapman; from the eccentric punk band Devo ("Whip It") to soul groups Kool & the Gang, the Ohio Players, and the O-Jays.

So it's fitting that Ohio is home to the glittering Rock & Roll Hall of Fame and Museum. The I. M. Pei–designed complex on the shore of Lake Erie in downtown Cleveland opened to great fanfare in 1995. The Hall of Fame honors the legendary figures of rock; its annual ceremony is one of the hottest tickets in the land. Inducted artists are featured in the Museum, which contains a computerized "jukebox" with virtually every song of every honoree—not to mention artifacts like the King's army uniform, Hank Williams's cowboy hat, and John Lennon's report card.

Devo. *Photofest. Left:* The Cars, one of the most successful New Wave bands of the late 1970s and early 1980s, had Ohio roots. Bassist Benjamin Orr, from Cleveland, met singer-guitarist Ric Ocasek (raised mostly in Ohio) at a party in Columbus. *Photofest*

Little Girl in Red Dress by Frank Duveneck, c. 1890. *Private Collection, Courtesy Keny Galleries, Columbus*

For much of the 19th century, Ohio was the primary source of artistic activity west of the Alleghenies. The state produced a myriad of major American painters, some of whom were content to paint their native surroundings, while more restless souls roamed the world. Among the former were genre painters John Henry Beard and Allan Smith, Jr., Cleveland's Archibald Willard (whose *Spirit of '76* is an American icon), and a group of painters who devoted themselves to the Ohio River landscape. These included the great African-American painter Robert S. Duncanson of the Hudson River School, and his colleagues William Sonntag and Worthington Whittredge. Ohio's most influential expatriate was Frank Duveneck, Kentucky-born but a Cincinnati resident when he went to study and paint in Munich in 1869. He was soon joined by a circle of young Cincinnati-area artists including Kenyon Cox, John Twachtman, and Joseph DeCamp, who became known as the "Duveneck Boys." Like their mentor, some later returned home to paint and teach, but others adopted a

peripatetic lifestyle. A later generation of Ohioans turned their artistic sights westward: John Hauser, Joseph Henry Sharp, Fernand Lungren, and illustrator Henry T. Farny all succumbed to the romance of the frontier.

Duck Hunters on the Ohio River by William Louis Sonntag, 1850. *Christie's Images*

Most of the key movements in art during the first half of the 20th century found exponents in Ohio. American Impressionism is well represented by Frederick Carl Gottwald and William Sommer of Cleveland, Henry Lewis Meakin of Cincinnati, and Alice Schille of Columbus (another expatriate and prodigal); rugged realism by

Untitled (Summer) by
William Zorach, 1914.
Private Collection

Gerrit Beneker's portraits of "worker-heroes" for the Navy Department. The highly personal regionalism of Charles Burchfield verges on Expressionism. Lithuanian immigrant William Zorach created modernist oil paintings whose pure, intense color suggest inspiration from Matisse; later he became better known for his sculpture. Cleveland's Raphael Gleitsmann was an inventive painter who fused modernist and regionalist imagery, as in his remarkable *The White Dam*, while the watercolor-and-graphite drawings of urban scenes by Lawrence Blazey echo the Ashcan School. And as documentary photojournalism was coming to the fore in the 1920s, the young Margaret Bourke-White made her reputation with powerful images of Cleveland's cityscape. 🏈

Main Street, Salem, Winter Day by Charles E. Burchfield, 1917–c. 1943. *Private Collection*
Above: The Jazz Bowl by Victor Schreckengost, c. 1930, Cowan Pottery. Ceramicist Viktor Schreckengost was a leader among several Ohioans who helped bring crafts into the realm of fine art in the mid-20th century. *Cleveland Museum of Art*

Ohio's contemporary arts scene is thriving, thanks to a few key institutions that foster and exhibit work by internationally known and native-born artists. The Cleveland Museum of Art occasionally showcases newer work; the Cleveland Institute of Art is a much-respected school; and the Cleveland Center for Contemporary Art (formerly the New Gallery) has shown cutting-edge visual art at several locations since 1968. The Contemporary Art Center in Cincinnati, founded in 1939 as one of the Midwest's first resources for modern art, is newly housed in an 80,000 square-foot facility downtown. At the Ohio State campus in Columbus, the prestigious Wexner Center for the Arts exhibits work in traditional media as well as film/video, multimedia, and performance art; and it sponsors resident artists, who often leave work behind—such as Athens native Maya Lin's 1993 installation *Groundswell.* The Dayton Visual Arts Center supports and shows artists from southern Ohio including video artist Jud Yalkut.

Currently Ohio's brightest name in the art world is Lima-born Ann Hamilton, who trained outside the state but has lived in Columbus since 1992. Her large-scale, labor-intensive installations have been shown at the Museum of Modern Art in New York and London's Tate Gallery, among other venues, and she was chosen to rep-

resent the U.S. at the Venice Biennale in 2000. Other Ohio-born artists who made their names elsewhere include Jim Dine (whose *Cincinnati Venus* highlights a downtown plaza); Kim Abeles, who studied at the University of Ohio; and prominent minimalist Robert Mangold. 🏈

Untitled (Topographic Landscape) **by Maya Lin, 1997. Columbus Museum of Art. Courtesy Gagosian Gallery, N.Y.**

"THE SPACESHIP THAT CRASH-LANDED ON THE PRAIRIES. . . ."

Performance artist Spalding Gray, describing the Wexner Center for the Arts,
designed by Peter Eisenman and Columbus architect Richard Trott

Big Clock in Little Switzerland

The Swiss heritage is strong in Ohio's Amish country, nowhere more so than at the Alpine-Alpa Swiss Market & Restaurant, on Rt. 62 outside Wilmot. There you can see the World's Largest Cuckoo Clock, which took 12 years to make and stands 23½ feet high, 24 feet long, and 13½ feet wide. Its hand-carved musical band and dancing couple perform every hour and half hour between April and Thanksgiving.

In Praise of Clean Living

If Cleveland's Museum of Health and Hygiene isn't quite the temple of oddness it was prior to a 1998 renovation, surviving exhibits do include the World's Largest Tooth and the Transparent Woman, a.k.a. Juno—a life-size see-through model with a hydraulic circulatory system and major organs. An exact replica of a 28-year-old woman, she was created by German refugee Franz Tsahackert, who worked in Dresden's German Hygiene Museum before fleeing the Communists in 1950. Push a button and Juno slowly rotates and narrates for ten minutes. Another popular attraction is the Theater of Human Sexuality. Gift shop souvenirs include finger-bone pens and spinal-column key rings.

Building a Better Basket

Looming surreally over southeastern Ohio's farmland is the headquarters of the Longaberger Company in Newark, a seven-story building shaped and detailed to resemble one of the company's famous market baskets. (Longaberger baskets are sold via home parties; they're a hot item on the eBay online auction site.) Longaberger's manufacturing campus in Dresden, 18 miles away, features the World's Largest Basket, the size of a small house and a can't-miss photo op.

Dublin's Big Ears

In the front yard of a Dublin insurance company, Columbus artist Malcolm Cochran created *Field of Corn (with Osage Orange Trees)*, more familiarly known as "the big ears of corn." Each about six feet tall, the 106 ears molded of white cement seem to have sprouted from the earth fully formed.

The piece is one of five Art in Public Places exhibits in and around Dublin.

Small-Town Savvy

Ashville calls itself the "small town capital of Ohio" and backs up the claim with a museum. Housed in a Scioto Valley Railroad station (1875), the Small Town Museum is a quirky collection of local history, nostalgia, and brushes with fame. Here, it's claimed, is the world's oldest traffic light, brought outside each July Fourth and hung at the corner of Harrison and Walnut. Other exhibits pay homage to Buster, the dog that voted Republican, Billy Carter, Tecumseh, Elvis, Sally Kellerman, Roy Rogers, and other personalities with ties to Ashville.

Wild Blue Yonders

The United States Air Force Museum at the Wright-Patterson Air Force Base, northeast of Dayton, displays some 300 aircraft in three giant hangars, with more on the vast swath of tarmac outside. They include a Stealth fighter, an SR-71 Blackbird, and several incarnations of Air Force One, including the first, used by Franklin Roosevelt and known as *Sacred Cow*. The Space Gallery features moon rocks, old space program gear, and products derived from space research, such as Velcro, CDs, and Tang. A World War I–era exhibit honors the stuffed "Stumpy John," an Air Force carrier pigeon.

Great People

A selective listing of native Ohioans, concentrating on the arts. (See page 54 for Ohio presidents.)

Theda Bara (1889–1955), actress

Sherwood Anderson (1876–1941), writer, best known for *Winesburg, Ohio*

Neil Armstrong (b. 1930), astronaut, first to set foot on moon

Erma Bombeck (1927–1996), humor columnist who celebrated the "mad housewife"

Hart Crane (1899–1932), poet, best known for *The Bridge*

George Armstrong Custer (1839–1876), officer in Civil War and Indian wars

Clarence Darrow (1857–1938), attorney, gained fame for Scopes Trial defense

Doris Day (b. 1924), singer and actress

Thomas A. Edison (1847–1931), inventor

Clark Gable (1901–1960), screen idol

John Glenn (b. 1921), astronaut, first American to orbit Earth

Robert Henri (1865–1929), artist, founder of Ashcan School

Toni Morrison (b. 1931), novelist, won Pulitzer Prize for *Beloved*

Paul Newman (b. 1925), actor

Jack Nicklaus (b. 1940), professional golf legend

Annie Oakley (1860–1926), sharpshooter and entertainer

Jesse Owens (1913–1980), track-and-field phenomenon, four-time Olympic gold medalist

Eddie Rickenbacker (1890–1973), aviator, WWI hero

Roy Rogers (1912–1998), singing cowboy actor

Pete Rose (b. 1941), baseball's all-time leader in hits

William T. Sherman (1820–1891), Civil War general

Steven Spielberg (b. 1947), movie magnate

Gloria Steinem (b. 1934), writer, feminist icon

Art Tatum (1910–1956), jazz pianist

Tecumseh (1768–1813), Shawnee chief, sided with British in War of 1812

James Thurber (1894–1961), writer, illustrator, and humorist

Victoria Woodhull (1838–1927), stockbroker, reformer, and 1872 presidential candidate for Equal Rights party

Orville (1871–1948) and **Wilbur** (1867–1912) **Wright**, aviation pioneers, invented first self-propelled airplane

Cy Young (1867–1955), baseball pitcher, all-time leader in games won

. . . and Great Places

Some interesting derivations of Ohio place names.

Akron Greek for "summit"; the city stands at the high point of a canal route to Lake Erie.

Bolivar Named for the Latin American patriot Simon Bolivar.

Brilliant Southern Ohio town named in early days of electric power; kin to other U.S. towns like Xray, Phoneton, Electron, and Radium.

Chagrin Falls Town and river in NE Ohio; said to have been named by Moses Cleaveland and his surveyors, embarrassed to have mistaken this river for the Cuyahoga.

Chillicothe (Say "Chil-uh-caw-thee.") Means "important town" in Shawnee; city on the Scioto was once Ohio's capital.

Cincinnati Named for the Roman republican hero Cincinnatus by General St. Clair in 1790.

Cleveland Founded by Connecticut General Moses Cleaveland on a parcel of Lake Erie frontage he bought after the Revolutionary War.

Fly Tiny Ohio Valley village so named because early settlers wanted a simple name.

Gallipolis Ohio's third oldest settlement, founded on the Ohio by French immigrants.

Gnadenhutten German for "tents of grace"; founded by Christian-convert Indians who were later massacred by U.S. militia.

Mahoning River From a Delaware word meaning "at the salt lick." From the same word came Licking Creek, near Cincinnati.

Marietta Oldest town in Ohio, named for Marie Antoinette of France.

Mingo Junction Town near Steubenville once inhabited by Mingo Indians, a West Virginia tribe.

Rio Grande A town and college just north of the Ohio River, the "rio grande" in this case.

Toledo Following a fashion for Spanish and Italian names, officials in 1833 chose this for the combined settlements of Port Lawrence and Vistula, after merchant Willard J. Daniels argued it "is easy to pronounce, is pleasant in sound, and there is no other city of that name on the American continent."

Twinsburg East of Cleveland; land for village square was donated by twins Aaron and Moses Wilcox.

Vermilion Resort town on Lake Erie, also Vermilion River; both named for the local red clay used by Ottawa Indians for paint.

Oberlin Town and college named for Jean Frederic Oberlin, an Alsatian clergyman and philanthropist (1740–1826) who labored for the poor.

OHIO BY THE SEASONS
A Perennial Calendar of Events and Festivals

Here is a selective listing of events that take place each year in the months noted;
we suggest calling ahead to local chambers of commerce for dates and details.

January

Canton
McKinley Day
Celebrates the birthday of the
25th president at the McKinley
Museum.

Chesterland
Winterfest
Snow volleyball, bikini slalom
are among the events at Alpine
Valley Ski Area.

February

Cadiz
Clark Gable's Birthday
Annual dinner dance in the
movie star's hometown.

Malabar Farm State Park
Evening Owl Walks

Roscoe Village
Ice Carving Festival

March

Cleveland
*Cleveland International Film
Festival*

Hinckley Township
Buzzard Sunday
Locals mark the birds' annual
return to Whipp's Ledges with a
pancake breakfast and art fair.

April

Medina
*Buckeye State Button Collectors
Show*

Rockbridge
Ohio Spring Classic Bicycle Races

May

Athens
Spring Literary Festival
Three-day event at Ohio U.
campus features nationally
known writers.

Cleveland
Cleveland Performance Art Festival
Performance artists show their
stuff at downtown's Colonial
Arcade.

*Rock and Roll Hall of Fame
Induction Ceremony*
Gathering of stars to be hon-
ored, and eager fans.

New Straitsville
Moonshine Festival
See a working still, hear traditional music, and consume
"moonshine" foods.

Port Clinton
Walleye Festival
Booths, rides, and more at this
celebration of Lake Erie's signa-
ture fish in Water Works Park.

June

Akron
AA Founder's Day Celebration
Held annually since 1935, the
event takes place on the
University of Akron campus.

Cleveland
Parade the Circle Celebration
Parade and all-day arts festival
presented by the cultural and
educational institutions of
University Circle.

Columbus
Columbus Arts Festival
Among the nation's top outdoor juried art shows; 300
exhibitors.

Defiance
Black Swamp Steam & Gas Show
Demonstrations of old-time
steam- and gas-powered equip-
ment at AuGlaize Village.

Oregonia
Fort Ancient Celebration
Native American events with a
prehistoric twist at this important Hopewell Culture site.

July

Canton
Pro Football Hall of Fame Festival
Speeches by inductees, plus the
season's first exhibition game.

Cleveland
Cleveland Race Week
One of the nation's largest fresh-water regattas, at Edgewater Yacht Club.

Crooksville
Crooksville–Roseville Pottery Festival
Important show and sale of collectible Ohio-made ceramics.

Toledo
LaGrange Street Polish Festival
All things Polish, including food, bands, polkas, and crafts.

August

Akron
All-American Soap Box Derby

Bucyrus
Bratwurst Festival
Vast array of recipes for the succulent brat.

Columbus
Ohio State Fair
One of the nation's largest fairs combines agricultural and show-business attractions; held over 17 days at Columbus Fairgrounds.

Kirtland
Vintage Ohio
Two dozen wineries and various restaurants provide wine and delicacies for sampling.

North Ridgeville
Corn Festival
The main draw is Amish-style roasted corn.

Toledo
Northwest Ohio Rib-Off
Prize-winning regional and national barbecue dishes, plus entertainment.

Twinsburg
Twins Days Festival
World's largest annual gathering of twins, as *Guinness Book of World Records* attests.

September

Cleveland
Head of the Cuyahoga Rowing Regatta

Lisbon
Johnny Appleseed Festival
Celebration honors apple messiah John Chapman and his favorite fruit.

Marietta
Ohio River Sternwheeler Festival

Sugarcreek
Ohio Swiss Festival
This village is ground zero for alpine culture in Ohio. Yodeling contest, of course.

October

Cincinnati
Gold Star Chilifest
Features nationally known country music acts plus infinite variations on the city's favorite dish.

Circleville
Circleville Pumpkin Show
This four-day gala is more than 90 years old.

Piqua
Great Outdoor Underwear Festival
Piqua once produced underwear; now citizens flaunt it at a celebrity underwear auction and the Undy 500 footrace.

Waynesville
Ohio Sauerkraut Festival
400-plus booths with crafts and food. Sauerkraut novelties include pizza, pie, and fudge.

November

Canton
Christkindl Market
Crafts, food, and fashions at Canton's Cultural Center for the Arts.

Tiffin
Tiffin Glass Collectors Club Show & Sale

December

Akron
Christmas at Stan Hywet
The lavish estate is decked from top to toe; madrigal dinners.

Cincinnati
Balluminaria
A dozen hot-air balloons hover above Eden Park's Mirror Lake, creating gorgeous reflections.

Lebanon
Historic Lebanon Christmas Festival

Perrysville
Christmas at Malabar Farm State Park
Country Christmas food and activities in a sylvan setting.

WHERE TO GO
Museums, Attractions, Gardens, and Other Arts Resources

Call for seasons and hours when open.

Museums

AKRON ART MUSEUM
70 E. Market St., Akron, 330-376-9185
A converted Renaissance Revival post office houses wide-ranging collections; photography is especially strong.

NEIL ARMSTRONG AIR & SPACE MUSEUM
I-75 Exit 11, Waponetka, 419-738-8811
Relics from Armstrong's moon voyage and other astronaut paraphernalia and displays.

BUTLER INSTITUTE OF AMERICAN ART
524 Wick Ave., Youngstown, 330-743-1711
Major American art collection includes Homer, Hopper, Sargent, and other notables.

CAMPUS MARTIUS MUSEUM
Second & Washington Sts., Marietta, 740-373-3750
Federal-style building houses artifacts and displays about early Ohio settlers and mound-builder cultures.

CINCINNATI ART MUSEUM
953 Eden Park Dr., 513-721-5204
Permanent collections and changing exhibitions; world's largest collection of Frank Duveneck works.

CINCINNATI MUSEUM CENTER
1301 Western Ave., Cincinnati, 513-287-7000
Housed in the restored Union Terminal are a historical museum and library, museum of natural history, children's museum, and Omnimax theater.

CLEVELAND CENTER FOR CONTEMPORARY ART
8501 Carnegie Ave., Cleveland, 216-421-8671
Long-established gallery for avant-garde art.

CLEVELAND MUSEUM OF ART
11150 East Blvd., Cleveland, 216-421-7340
Classical building in University Circle holds 70 galleries, 34,000 works in permanent collection, major traveling shows; strong in antiquities and American paintings.

COLUMBUS MUSEUM OF ART
480 E. Broad St., Columbus, 614-221-6801
Permanent and changing exhibitions in all media; features European and American paintings, sculpture, ethnic art.

DAYTON ART INSTITUTE
456 Belmont Park N., Dayton, 937-223-5277
One of the nation's best mid-sized museums in a recently renovated Romanesque sandstone building; outstanding Asian collection.

MCKINLEY MUSEUM
800 McKinley Monument Dr. NW, Canton, 330-455-7043
Diverse complex includes a museum of science and industry, planetarium, and McKinley National Monument.

MOTORCYCLE HERITAGE MUSEUM
33 Collegeview Rd., Westerville, 614-882-2782
Run by American Motorcycle Association; displays vintage bikes on loan. Not far away, in Pickering, is the similar Motorcycle Hall of Fame Museum.

OHIO RIVER MUSEUM
601 Front St., Marietta, 740-373-3750
Devoted to Ohio River history; incorporates the steamboat W. P. Snyder, Jr., anchored nearby.

ROCK AND ROLL HALL OF FAME AND MUSEUM
1 Key Plaza, Cleveland, 216-781-7625
The I. M. Pei–designed museum is now the state's premier attraction; features innovative exhibitions and occasional performances.

TAFT MUSEUM
316 Pike St., Cincinnati, 513-241-0343
The building itself is important—Ohio's best Federal-style mansion—as are the treasures it holds, including paintings, furnishings, and decorative arts.

TOLEDO MUSEUM OF ART
2445 Monroe St., Toledo, 419-255-8000
Ranks among the nation's top museums; collections from antiquity to contemporary arts, including extensive glass works. Frank Gehry designed a 1992 addition, the University of Toledo Center for Visual Arts.

U.S. AIR FORCE MUSEUM
Wright Patterson Air Force Base, Dayton, 937-255-3286
More than 300 aircraft and missiles, several Air Force One planes, and an IMAX theater.

WESTERN RESERVE HISTORICAL SOCIETY
10825 East Blvd., Cleveland, 216-751-5722
Exhibits highlight northeast Ohio history, including a Gilded Age mansion; there's also an auto-aviation museum with 150-plus vintage cars.

WEXNER CENTER FOR THE ARTS
North High St. at 15th Ave., Columbus, 614-292-3235
Showcases contemporary arts in all media, on the Ohio U. campus.

Attractions

CENTER OF SCIENCE AND INDUSTRY (COSI)
333 W. Broad St., Columbus, 614-228-COSI
Pioneer in hands-on learning has huge new riverfront home designed by Arata Isosaki. Aquarium, natural history museum, and science center combined, it also houses the 7-story IWERKS Extreme Screen Theater. COSI Toledo is a satellite operation.

DAYTON AVIATION HERITAGE NATIONAL HISTORICAL PARK
Various Dayton locations, 937-225-7705
Four sites include the Wright Brothers bicycle shop and Carillon Park, home to the 1905 *Wright Flyer III.*

FORT ANCIENT STATE MEMORIAL
6123 Ohio 350, Oregonia, 513-932-4421
Another important Native American site; includes state-of-the-art museum and trails.

GERMAN VILLAGE
Downtown Columbus
Historic district recreates German neighborhood of the 1880s, with brick streets, period buildings, theme dining.

GOODYEAR WORLD OF RUBBER
1144 E. Market St., Akron, 330-796-7117
Charles Goodyear's workshop, racing cars, and tires, of course, including some that rolled over the moon.

GREAT LAKES SCIENCE CENTER
601 Erieside, Cleveland, 216-694-2000
More than 300 hands-on exhibits, plus an Omnivax theater.

INVENTURE PLACE
221 S. Broadway, Akron, 330-762-4463
The National Inventors Hall of Fame, which the *Wall Street Journal* calls "a Cooperstown for gadgeteers and tinkerers."

LAKE FARMPARK

8800 Chardon Rd. (U.S. 6), Kirtland, 440-256-2122

Open-air science and cultural center with focus on livestock breeding and Ohio farming.

PRO FOOTBALL HALL OF FAME

2121 George Halas Dr., Canton, 330-456-8207

Mecca for football fans, especially during the Hall of Fame Festival in July.

SCHOENBRUNN VILLAGE STATE MEMORIAL

East High Ave. (SR 259), New Philadelphia, 330-339-3636

Carefully reconstructed 18th-century village at Ohio's first Christian settlement.

SERPENT MOUND STATE MEMORIAL

45 mi. SW of Chillicothe, U.S. 50, 413-587-2796

Largest serpent effigy mound in North America, created around 1070 A.D.

SUNWATCH ARCHAEOLOGICAL PARK

2301 W. River Rd., Dayton, 937-268-8199

Reconstructed village from the Fort Ancient culture, with excellent interpretive displays.

TECUMSEH!

Sugarloaf Mountain Amphitheater, Delano Marietta Rd., Chillicothe, 740-775-0700

Perhaps the best of Ohio's outdoor summer dramas; highlights the career of the great Shawnee chief.

ZOAR VILLAGE

Twelve-block historic district illustrates the communal lifestyle of German immigrants who settled here.

Homes and Gardens

ADENA STATE MEMORIAL

848 Adena Rd., Chillicothe, 740-772-1500

The 1807 estate of Thomas Worthington, Ohio's sixth governor, has period furnishings and outbuildings.

DR. BOB'S HOME

885 Ardmore Ave., Akron, 330-864-1935

Home of the co-founder of Alcoholics Anonymous; memorabilia and library.

DUNBAR HOUSE STATE MEMORIAL

219 Paul Laurence Dunbar St., Dayton, 513-224-7061

Poet Paul Laurence Dunbar's restored home is the first publicly owned African-American historic site.

EDISON BIRTHPLACE MUSEUM

9 Edison Dr., Milan, 419-499-2135

Three-story brick house where Edison lived until age 7 contains examples of his early experiments.

FRANKLIN PARK CONSERVATORY AND BOTANICAL GARDEN

1777 E. Broad St., Columbus, 614-645-8733

Beautiful oasis in downtown; conservatory showcases botanical zones from desert to Pacific atoll.

GLENDOWER STATE MEMORIAL

Orchard Ave. (U.S. 42), Lebanon, 513-932-1817

Outstanding Greek Revival home (1836) on a hilltop is furnished with pioneer artifacts from the area.

HOLDEN ARBORETUM

9500 Sperry Rd., Kirtland, 440-946-4400

Largest arboretum in U.S., 3,100 acres of fields, forests, ponds, and gardens, plus 20 miles of trails.

MALABAR FARM STATE PARK

4050 Bromfield Rd., Lucas, 419-892-2784

Writer Louis Bromfield lived here from 1939–1956, farming, preserving nature, and entertaining the cultural elite (Bogey and Bacall were married here); tours of the Big House and grounds, hiking, etc.

RANKIN HOUSE STATE MEMORIAL

Rankin Hill Rd., Ripley, 513-392-1627

Preserved 1828 home of abolitionist John Rankin was a key Underground Railroad station.

SECREST ARBORETUM

1680 Madison Ave. (SR 302), Wooster, 330-263-3779

Major arboretum and rose garden at the 2,100-acre Ohio Agricultural Research and Development Center.

STAN HYWET HALL AND GARDENS

714 N. Portage Path, Akron, 330-836-5333

America's premier example of Tudor Revival architecture, built 1911–15, and 70 acres of magnificent gardens.

JAMES THURBER HOUSE

77 Jefferson Ave., Columbus, 614-464-1032

The small 1873 house where Thurber lived contains a library, memorabilia, and bookshop; often used for literary events.

WARTHER CARVINGS AND GARDENS

331 Karl Rd., Dover, 330-343-7513

The work of several generations of woodcarvers is displayed in this Amish home, set in acres of Swiss gardens.

WELTZHEIMER-JOHNSON HOUSE

127 Woodhaven Dr., Oberlin, 440-775-8665

Only Frank Lloyd Wright home in Ohio open to the public, his first attempt at Usonian design (1950).

YODER'S AMISH HOME

6050 SR 515, Millersburg, 330-893-2541

Guided tours of this Amish farm, including the family kitchen and bakery.

Other Resources

OHIO DIVISION OF TRAVEL AND TOURISM

1-800-BUCKEYE, www.ohiotourism.com

Features, travel advice, information packets, and extensive links on Web site.

OHIO HISTORICAL CENTER AND OHIO VILLAGE

1982 Velma Ave., Columbus, 614–297–2300

The Ohio Historical Society site: permanent and changing exhibitions in an impressive new building highlight state history and native cultures; the village recreates a Civil War–era town.

OHIO STATEHOUSE

Capitol Square, Columbus

Fine 1861 Greek Revival building, recently restored, connects via a new atrium to the historic Senate Building (1901).

CREDITS

The authors have made every effort to reach copyright holders of text and owners of illustrations, and wish to thank those individuals and institutions that permitted the reprinting of text or the reproduction of works in their collections. Credits not listed in the captions are provided below. References are to page numbers; the designations a, b, and c indicate position of illustrations on pages.

Text

"Ohio," from *Wonderful Town:* Leonard Bernstein, Betty Comden and Adolph Green. The Leonard Bernstein Music Publishing Company LLC, Universal Music Publishing Group. 2440 Sepulveda Blvd., Suite 100, Los Angeles, CA, 90064.

Illustrations

JIM BARON/IMAGES FINDERS: **89;** BUTLER MUSEUM OF AMERICAN ART, YOUNGSTOWN: **64a** *Pete Rose,* 1985. Color screen on white lenox paper. 38⅜ x 31½"; © Estate of Andy Warhol/ARS, N.Y.; **65** *Minor League,* 1946. Oil on canvas. 40 x 50"; CHICAGO NATURAL HISTORY MUSEUM: **28a** Oil on canvas; Christie's Images: **18–19** *Mill Creek Valley, Cincinnati,* n.d. Oil on canvas; **20** *Ohio River Near Marietta,* 1855. Oil on canvas; **38** *The White Dam,* 1939. Oil on canvas. 38½ x 43½"; **81** *Duck Hunters on the Ohio River,* 1850. Oil on canvas; CINCINNATI ART MUSEUM: **32a** *The Underground Railroad,* 1893. Oil on canvas. 52³⁄₁₆ x 76⅛". Subscription fund purchase; CLEVELAND MUSEUM OF ART: **83a** *The Jazz Bowl* (or New Yorker), 1931. Glazed ceramic. 28.6 x 41.3 cm. John L. Severance Fund; COLUMBUS MUSEUM OF ART: **85** *Untitled (Topographic Landscape),* 1997. Particle board. 16 x 18½'. Museum Purchase, Derby Fund. Courtesy Gagosian Gallery, N.Y.; CULVER PICTURES: **88;** DAYTON ART INSTITUTE: **41c** Ceramic vase with metallic luster glaze, 1902. 17¾ x 5¼". Gift of Stephen Fales, 1983; Collection of Joseph M. and Elsie Erdelac: **10** *Horsedrawn Cart in Thunderstorm,* 1918. Oil on board. 20 x 25½"; **12** *U.S. Mail/Brandywine Landscape,* 1938 (detail). Watercolor. 35⅞ x 20⅞"; **25** *Lake Erie Cliff, Lakewood,* 1911. Oil on canvas. 24 x 20"; HENRY FRANCIS DU PONT WINTERTHUR MUSEUM: **31b** *Anthony Wayne,* early 1800s. Oil on board. 9⅞ x 7⅝"; THE INLANDER COLLECTION OF GREAT LAKES REGIONAL PAINTING: **36a** *Freighters,* 1931. Oil on canvas. 35¼ x 41¼"; COURTESY THE KENNEDY GALLERIES: **44** *Safety Valve,* 1921. Watercolor on paper. 20 x 30". Private Collection; COURTESY KENY GALLERIES, COLUMBUS: **57b** *A Summer Day,* 1915. Oil on canvas. 25 x 30". Private Collection; **61** *Sewing in the Garden,* c. 1915. Oil on canvas. 35¼ x 28¼". Private Collection; **80** *Little Girl in Red Dress,* c. 1890. Oil on canvas. 26 x 21¾" Private Collection; MANOOGIAN COLLECTION: **2** *Ella's Hotel, Richfield Center,* Ohio, 1885. Oil on canvas. 31 x 42½"; National Geographic Image Collection: **12a** Marilyn Dye Smith; **12b** Robert Hynes; NATIONAL MUSEUM OF AMERICAN ART, SMITHSONIAN INSTITUTION/ART RESOURCE: **58** *Mount Healthy, Ohio,* 1844. Oil on canvas. 28 x 36¼". Gift of Leonard Granoff; OHIO DEPARTMENT OF TOURISM: **87b;** PHOTOFEST: **75b; 75c;** PRIVATE COLLECTION: **11** *Farm Near Canal,* 1935. Oil on board. 31¾ x 38½"; **82** *Untitled (Summer),* 1914. Oil on canvas. 31¾ x 36¾"; **83b** *Main Street, Salem,* c. 1943. Watercolor on paper. 36½ x 47½"; PRIVATE COLLECTION, LAURIE WINFREY, INC.: **39a** *Declarant,* 1919 Oil on canvas. 45.7 x 40.6 cm; COURTESY PROCTOR & GAMBLE, CINCINNATI: **9** *Ohio Valley and Kentucky Hills,* 1910. Oil on canvas. 40 x 52"; RANDALL SCHIEBER: **86a; 86b; 87b;** THE SCHOEN COLLECTION, MIAMI: **34** *Good Crop,* 1942. Oil on canvas. 43 x 29"; SOUTHERN OHIO MUSEUM, PORTSMOUTH: **71b** *Merry-Go-Round,* 1949. Oil on canvas. 21½ x 32¼". Gift of Dorothy W. Miller; TERRA FOUNDATION FOR THE ARTS: **47** *Lotus Lilies,* 1888. Oil on canvas. 18 x 32". Daniel J. Terra Collection

Acknowledgments

Grateful thanks are extended to Joyce and Karyn Gerhard and Margaret and Richard Wenstrup.